Lifestyle Math

Your Financial Planning Portfolio

A Supplemental Mathematics Unit
for **Career Choices**

by Mindy Bingham, Jo Willhite and Shirley Myers

Illustrated by Itoko Maeno and Janice Blair

Academic Innovations, Santa Barbara, California

My Financial Planning Portfolio

This book belongs to _____

Date started: _____

Date completed: _____

Published by Academic Innovations

www.academicinnovations.com
(800) 967-8016

Manufactured in the United States of America

25 24 23 22 21 20 19 18 17 16 15 14 13 12 11

Dear Reader,

You are about to embark on probably the most important math problem you will ever solve in your life. Actually, it is not just one but a series of math problems that lead you to the cost of the lifestyle you envision for yourself as an adult.

This figure is a critical ingredient in your decision about the kind of career you'd like and your willingness to prepare for it. Matching your lifestyle expectations with the financial realities of a job is essential to a satisfying life.

Please note! The first total in your "budget profile" may change, depending on how much time and energy you decide to commit to maintaining a particular lifestyle. Once you've completed this process, you will have the information and formulas to perform the revisions that may be necessary throughout your life.

If later you decide you don't want to commit yourself to the education and preparation required for a specific career, you will know the process for adjusting to changes in your personal expectations. In the future, should you change your lifestyle because, for example, you shift to another line of work or you want to stay home and raise your children, you will have the tools to adjust your financial plans.

Working through the challenge of the activities in this book and learning the formulas that you'll use repeatedly in the future will equip you with the tools to save money, stretch your resources, reduce frustration and broaden your choices. For nearly twenty years, high school and college students have consistently cited the problems in this book as favorite activities of our curriculum. Students report years later how meaningful and valuable this experience was in preparing them for "real life."

We hope you accept and enjoy this challenge as fully as those former students, but, before we begin, let's consider the psychology or the "inner game" of mathematics.

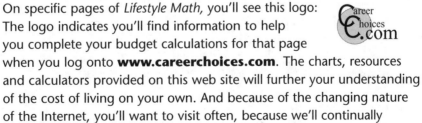

On specific pages of *Lifestyle Math,* you'll see this logo: The logo indicates you'll find information to help you complete your budget calculations for that page when you log onto **www.careerchoices.com**. The charts, resources and calculators provided on this web site will further your understanding of the cost of living on your own. And because of the changing nature of the Internet, you'll want to visit often, because we'll continually update and add new facts and tips.

Math is not a talent . . .

It is a skill to be learned

You may be thinking it doesn't seem that way to you. Maybe you struggle with numbers and, even if you don't struggle, perhaps you'd like to avoid math any time you can. You may have even felt or been told that math is just "not your subject."

Well, the truth is anyone can learn math!

During her high school and college years, **Career Choices** co-author Mindy Bingham tutored junior and senior high students in a variety of math subjects. One summer, Andy, a thirteen-year-old with severe learning disabilities, was her student. His family had been informed that the public school could no longer accommodate him and therefore he must enroll in a special school. Andy and his parents were distraught until a bargain was struck between Andy's family and the neighborhood middle school. If he could pass the eighth grade math exam required of all students the first week of school the following fall, he could remain with his class and friends.

Mindy and Andy worked all summer, two hours each day. Because Andy had very limited math skills, they needed to start at the beginning with addition and subtraction of whole numbers. Andy worked hard and practiced and drilled every day. As the summer continued, so did Andy — through fractions, decimals, ratios and beginning algebra. He was so motivated he worked on his problems on his own time.

His hard work paid off. Not only did Andy pass the test, but when the results were released, he held the second highest score among that group of 350 students.

A Skill to be Learned

Think about learning math skills the same way you would learn the skills to play basketball. First you start learning to handle the ball, dribble, toss and throw. There is no easy or magic way around this. It takes practice, practice, practice. Once you have perfected the basics, you begin learning to make baskets, starting close to the hoop and slowly moving further and further into the court as you practice to improve your shooting skill. Eventually you're starting to play. With each new game experience you continue to perfect your skill and develop your strategies. If you stick with it long enough, put in enough effort and energy, your work finally pays off and you join the basketball team. If you are a basketball player, you know how hard you worked to develop your skill.

The same is true for learning math. First you start by learning the basics: addition, subtraction, multiplication, and division of whole numbers, decimals and fractions. Step by step and practice, practice, practice. This was the focus of your math classes in elementary school.

Once you perfect the basics, you begin learning how to put these skills together to learn more complex functions. Just as in playing basketball, you must practice and perfect the basics in order to be in the game.

The game of life requires that you know the ways to use those basic skills of math. The life problems with which you will be working in this portfolio should convince you that math skills are essential to making the best choices for yourself. It is our hope that the following life problems will help to further convince you that *math knowledge is power.*

If you think you can, you can.

If you think you can't, you won't.

What Is Your Attitude about Math?

When you think about math class you
- ☐ feel confident about your ability to learn the material.
- ☐ feel anxious and wish you didn't have to take math.

When you start a new topic in math class you
- ☐ look forward to the challenge of broadening your understanding of math.
- ☐ are apprehensive and concerned you won't be able to keep up.

Which statement best describes why you are taking math?
- ☐ It offers me more options for my future.
- ☐ It is a required course for graduation.

Good math skills are
- ☐ a requirement for any worker in the age of technology.
- ☐ not something I need to acquire.

Your father or other significant male adult
- ☐ feels comfortable with his math abilities.
- ☐ feels uncomfortable with his math abilities.

Your mother or other significant female adult
- ☐ feels comfortable with her math abilities.
- ☐ feels uncomfortable with her math abilities.

Think of your grade school teachers. How did they feel
about your math abilities and what did they communicate to you?
- ☐ You are a good math student.
- ☐ You are not a good math student.

If you checked the first statement most often, your attitude will promote your learning of math. If you checked the second statement most often, you just might have the experiences and attitudes of someone with *math anxiety*, a condition that could hinder your ability to learn what is necessary for a successful future.

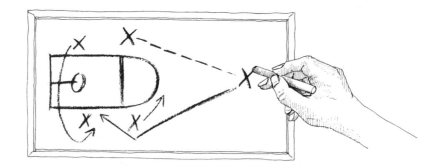

Math Anxiety:
What Is It?
What to Do about It.

It is curable!

The reason many students do not do well in math is a condition known as *math anxiety*. In other words, the mere thought or mention of math makes them anxious or uneasy. Because of this feeling, these individuals may not think they have the ability to learn math. Their belief then becomes a reality.

Why are some people fearful of math? The variety of reasons includes negative learning experiences in school, parents or peers who did not encourage that individual's math efforts, or parents who themselves have math anxiety.

Females are particularly prone to this anxiety and therefore resist pursuing math. This also occurs for various reasons. For instance, if the role models in their lives did not possess or value math skills, girls might copy that example. Girls who received less support from their teachers of mathematics or who were told by a counselor not to worry since they wouldn't need math are far less likely to challenge themselves. As long as girls are rewarded for their appearance and pleasing personality rather than their mental abilities, it's not hard to see where they will direct their efforts.

Whatever the reason, if you think you suffer from math anxiety, it won't help to point a finger at others for your problem. Since you are the one who will suffer from a lack of math skills, YOU are the one who must do something about the situation. The good news is that you can change the way you feel about math. With energy and awareness, you can remove the roadblocks of anxiety. Because of the power it gives you over your life decisions, you can learn to enjoy, embrace and value math.

So . . . . . .

If every time you think of math class, your heart starts to race or your hands get sweaty....

If, at class registration time, you think you'd do anything not to have to take math...

Turn to pages 216-221 in **Career Choices** and begin today to start changing your feelings about math. Practicing these helpful hints will empower you to become the independent, successful adult of your dreams.

Take charge of your thoughts.
You can do what you will with them.
— Plato

Getting Help

The math problems in this portfolio are based on some of the most important real-life choices you will make as a young adult. While they may look complicated, they are not. The math skills required to figure your own financial profile are the basic skills of:

addition, subtraction, multiplication, and division of whole numbers, decimals, and fractions.

You'll also practice the use of:

percentages, ratio and proportion, charts and graphs, estimation, measurement, and statistics.

Most importantly, this series of activities should help you understand how a solid math background can improve your life. Once you are confident in your knowledge of the basic skills, you should be able to proceed through the challenges of this portfolio with little assistance.

However, should you need practice or instruction in any of the basic skills, start to get help as you work through this book. While you may be tempted to ignore the fact that you don't know how to figure your down payment on the house or car you want to buy (multiplication of decimals and subtraction of whole numbers), let us assure you it will not go unnoticed by the bank loan officer you want to impress.

We encourage you to use the *Request for Assistance form* on the following page to communicate those needs to your instructor. If you're willing to put in the time and energy, you too can be proficient in math.

To make it easy for you to identify which skills you know and which ones you need to work on, icons appear on each page to show the skills each problem or activity requires. The following chart explains these symbols. Circle the functions in which you need more practice.

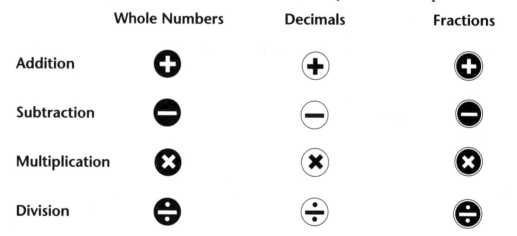

	Whole Numbers	Decimals	Fractions
Addition	➕	⊕	➕
Subtraction	➖	⊖	➖
Multiplication	✖	⊗	✖
Division	➗	⊘	➗

www.lifestylemath.com

Now you can also go to the Internet for help. Once you've completed your mathematical calculations for each activity, you'll want to check them to see if they are correct. Go to **www.lifestylemath.com** and log on with the ID name and password given to you by your instructor. Click on the page number you are working on and fill in your calculations from this *Lifestyle Math* workbook. This computerized correction aid will evaluate your work and indicate if it is correct. If it is not, it will point out where in the process your calculations are wrong, so you can go back and rework them. You can visit this website from home, school, or the library.

Request for Assistance in Learning from My Instructor

To: _____ date _____
        Instructor's name

From: _____ date _____
          Student's name

I would like to request help with the following math skills;

Whole numbers:

☐ Addition ☐ Subtraction ☐ Multiplication ☐ Division

Decimal/Percentage:

☐ Addition ☐ Subtraction ☐ Multiplication ☐ Division

Fractions:

☐ Addition ☐ Subtraction ☐ Multiplication ☐ Division

☐ **Percentages**

☐ **Ratio and proportion**

☐ **Charts and graphs**

☐ **Estimation**

☐ **Measurement**

☐ **Statistics**

I am particularly stumped with the following problem. (Describe the problem below.):

_____

_____

_____

MY COMMITMENT TO MY LEARNING

To improve my skills I am willing to: (Check all that you will commit to.)

☐ Meet with you at lunch breaks.

☐ Meet with you after school or work.

☐ Attend special session in and out of class.

☐ Work independently at the computer lab.

☐ Complete practice worksheets as homework.

☐ Other _____

What Does That Word Mean?

Perhaps some of the terms in this workbook are unfamiliar to you. Here are definitions of many of the new words you are now adding to your vocabulary because you have undertaken to plan wisely for your future.

AFFORDABLE: Within one's financial means.

AMORTIZATION: The repayment of a debt, including interest, usually in monthly installments which continue until the loan is paid in full.

ANNUAL: Yearly, every year.

BUDGET: An itemized list of expected income and expenses for a given period of time; the total sum of money set aside for a given purpose.

COMPENSATION: Payment given or received in return for work

DEPRECIATION: A decrease in value due to wear and tear, decay, decline in price, etc.; the difference between the original cost and the resale price or book value.

DOWN PAYMENT: An initial amount paid at the time of purchase in installment buying.

ESTIMATE: A judgment or opinion based on very general considerations; an approximate calculation.

FORMULA: A rule or principle frequently expressed in mathematical language; a set form indicating procedure to be followed.

GROSS PAY: Total compensation before deductions.

ICON: A sign; picture or symbol.

INDEX: Any sequential arrangement of material; adjustment of wages, taxes, etc. according to changes in the cost of living or some other economic indicator.

LIFESTYLE: The habits, attitudes, tastes, standards, economic level, etc., that constitute the mode of living of an individual or group.

LOAN: A sum of money lent with interest to be included as part of repayment.

MORTGAGE: A conveyance of property to a creditor as security for money lent.

NET PAY: The amount remaining of the pay received after all deductions have
         been withheld (take home pay).

PAYROLL DEDUCTIONS: Amount withheld from gross pay for federal
         and state income taxes, Social Security, pension or savings,
         unemployment and health care insurance, workers'
         compensation, etc.

PENSION: A fixed amount paid regularly by a former employer to a
         retired person and his/her dependents.

QUANTITATIVE: Describing or measuring quantity.

RESTRUCTURE: To rebuild; to bring about a fundamental change in an
         organization, system, etc.

SALARY: A fixed compensation paid to a person for regular work or services.

SPREADSHEET: A computer produced worksheet arranged in columns
         (mathematical matrix).

Below write any other financial terms you learn as you work through your personal plan.

What Cost This Lifestyle?

As a class, debate the following question:

Should you make a career choice and then adjust your lifestyle to fit the salary of that career? Or should you choose a lifestyle, evaluate its costs and then select a career attainable to you that supports that lifestyle.

Read pages 76 & 77 of **Career Choices**.

After thinking about what you visualize your life to be like at age 29, complete the following family profile.

FAMILY PROFILE

MARITAL STATUS	CHILDREN	AGES OF CHILDREN
☐ Single	☐ 0	_____
☐ Married	☐ 1	_____
☐ Divorced	☐ 2	_____
☐ Separated	☐ 3	_____
☐ Widowed	☐ 4	_____
☐ Other	☐ 5	_____
	☐ 6	_____
	☐ 7	_____

WHERE I WOULD LIKE TO LIVE _____

WHY? _____

O.K. You are ready to begin.

THE TASK

Come up with a budget for the way you want to live when you are 29 years old.

Your Budget Profile

The Monthly Expenses of Your Desired Lifestyle When You are 29 Years Old.

You'll refer back and complete this page throughout the course.

Housing

Payment/rent	$ _____	[1.1]
Property taxes	$ _____	[1.2]
Insurance	$ _____	[1.3]
Total utilities	$ _____	[1.4]
Telephone	$ _____	[1.5]

Housing $ _____ [1]

Transportation

Car payments	$ _____	[2.1]
Gasoline	$ _____	[2.2]
Maintenance and insurance	$ _____	[2.3]
Public transportation	$ _____	[2.4]

Transportation $ _____ [2]

Clothing

Your clothing	$ _____	[3.1]
Spouse's clothing	$ _____	[3.2]
Children's clothing	$ _____	[3.3]

Clothing $ _____ [3]

Food and
Sundries $ _____ [4]

Entertainment
and Recreation $ _____ [5]

Vacations $ _____ [6]

Child Care $ _____ [7]

Health Care $ _____ [8]

Furnishings $ _____ [9]

Savings $ _____ [10]

Miscellaneous $ _____ [11]

**Total Monthly Expenses
or Minimum Required
Monthly Net Pay** $ _____ **[12]**

See page 85 for page numbers where line totals can be found.

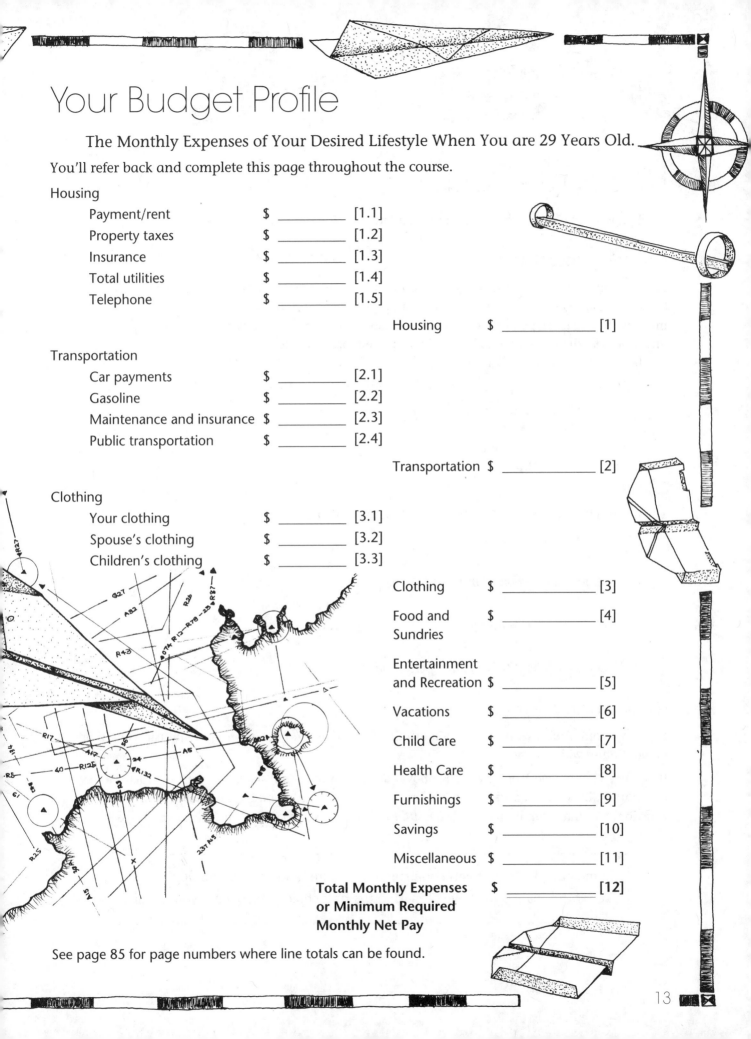

Housing Budget

Read page 78 of **Career Choices** and think about the kind of housing you desire.

Choosing Your Housing:

Pretend you are 29 years old and are trying to find housing. You must decide whether to rent or to purchase. Where you live is an important decision and should not be made without careful preparation and comparison. The more you study the figures and costs and the better you understand them, the more advantageous position you will be in to make the right choices for you and your family.

Complete all columns on page 17 as you work through this exercise.

A – Rental of an apartment
B – Rental of a house
C – Own a condominium
D – Own a house

The math skills required to make this important decision are:

Addition (*whole numbers and percentages*)

Subtraction (*whole numbers and percentages*)

Multiplication (*whole numbers and percentages*)

Division (*whole numbers and percentages*)

Getting Help

If you are comfortable with the above math functions, choosing the appropriate housing based on actual figures will be easy.

If you need help to work on any of the above math computational skills, ask your instructor to review the math skills with you and to give you practice problems until you feel competent with each function. You may want to use the *Request for Learning Assistance* forms beginning on page 9.

> Remember, the better you understand the figures and computational skills, the better the chance you have of making the best choice for you and your family.

How Personalized Do You Want the Budget of Your Described Lifestyle?

On the following pages you will be asked to complete several worksheets which, when completed, will project your housing costs for a variety of types of dwellings. Once you have chosen a specific dwelling for each category of housing (see page 16), complete the activities on pages 18 to 24 and then transfer your data to the MONTHLY HOUSING BUDGET WORKSHEET on page 17. You may want to research actual prices and percentages used in your state or area, or you may want to use the average figures given in this exercise.

Your research: If you decide to spend the extra time required to gather this individual data, you will be rewarded with a monthly figure that is very close to your actual costs, based on your expectations for housing.

Using an average figure: We have given you average figures, in case you don't have the time to gather more exact data to represent your own unique lifestyle.

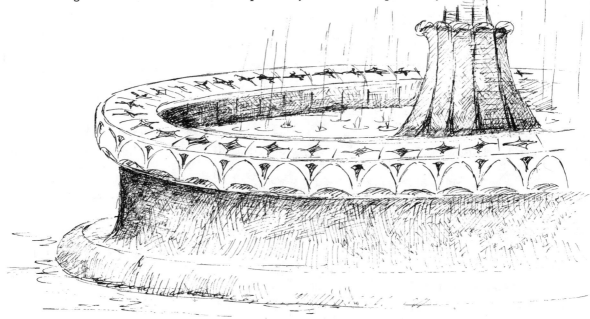

Do You Want to Own or Rent?

Your Local Housing Costs

Get a copy of your local newspaper's classified ad section and choose one example of housing that you think you would like to live in for each category of housing described below. Remember to keep in mind the needs of the family you described on page 12.

Paste the copy of the classified ad describing each desirable property below.

Rental Apartment	Rental House
Own Condominum	Own House

Describe your choices:

Rental Apartment   _____ # of bedrooms   _____ # of bathrooms

Rental House   _____ # of bedrooms   _____ # of bathrooms

Own Condo   _____ # of bedrooms   _____ # of bathrooms

Own House   _____ # of bedrooms   _____ # of bathrooms

Sometimes we have strong feelings about owning or renting a specific kind of dwelling. Before you make a purely emotional decision, it is wise to complete a comparison of the costs of various types of dwellings.

MONTHLY HOUSING BUDGET WORKSHEET

	A RENT APARTMENT	B RENT HOUSE	C OWN CONDO	D OWN HOUSE
1. Mortgage payment or monthly rent [1.1]				
2. Property taxes [1.2]	N/A*	N/A		
3. Insurance renter's/property [1.3]				
4. Homeowner's Association fees [1.3]	N/A	N/A		N/A
5. Total utilities [1.4]				
6. Telephone [1.5]				
Total Housing Costs [1]				

The chart above will help you compare the monthly costs for various housing choices. The next eight pages will provide the information needed to complete your MONTHLY HOUSING BUDGET WORKSHEET.

Once you choose your desired housing, enter the appropriate figures on page 13, lines 1.1 through 1.5.

*N/A means *Not Applicable.* For instance the person renting an apartment does not pay property taxes.

Renting or Owning

Your research: If you want to learn the actual prices in your area, you can start with the classified section of your newspaper or go online using your favorite search engine. Just type in the words "real estate" and the city name to find the current listings. Choose properties to own or rent that sound appealing and realistic for your plans when you are 29 years old.

Using an average figure: Turn to pages 28 and 29 for average home costs throughout the U.S.

Renting

Most classified ads for rental property list the monthly rent. Put the figure for the apartment you chose in column A, line 1 on page 17.

Owning

The monthly mortgage payment is based upon the property's price, the down payment, the interest rate and the length of the loan. Your mortgage payment is not difficult to compute if you follow the formula. Here is how it is done:

First figure the down payment required.

For example, a two-bedroom condominium in the Midwest averages $120,000. If you are purchasing such a condo and a 20% (.20) down payment is required, your down payment would be $24,000.

$$
\begin{array}{rl}
\$120,000 & \text{purchase price} \\
\underline{\textbf{X} \quad .20} & \text{\% down payment required} \\
\$ \ 24,000 & \text{down payment}
\end{array}
$$

Now find the amount to be financed.

The balance of $96,000 (found by substracting the down payment from the purchase price) would be the amount of money left to be financed by the bank.

$$
\begin{array}{rl}
\$120,000 & \textit{purchase price} \\
\underline{- \ \$24,000} & \textit{down payment required} \\
\$ \ 96,000 & \textit{amount to be financed}
\end{array}
$$

Figuring Monthly Mortgage Payments

Interest Rate	Monthly payment per $1,000 for 30-year fixed-rate mortgage	Interest Rate	Monthly payment per $1,000 for 30-year fixed-rate mortgage
4%	$4.77	8%	$7.34
4½%	$5.07	8½%	$7.69
5%	$5.37	9%	$8.05
5½%	$5.68	9½%	$8.41
6%	$6.00	10%	$8.77
6½%	$6.32	10½%	$9.15
7%	$6.66	11%	$9.52
7½%	$6.99	11½%	$9.90

Use the chart to help you figure your monthly mortgage payment. For example, if you want to find the monthly payment for a $96,000, 30-year loan at 7%, multiply $6.66 by 96. The monthly mortgage payment would be $639.36. Here's how it's done.

STEP 1. Find out how many thousands are in the amount to be financed.

$$1{,}000 \overline{)\,\$\,96{,}000.00} = 96.00$$

Can you think of a quicker way of finding the number of thousands (1000s) in a number?

Find the number of 1000s for

$86,900   \underline{\hspace{4cm}}

$125,100   \underline{\hspace{4cm}}

$365,000   \underline{\hspace{4cm}}

$69,500   \underline{\hspace{4cm}}

STEP 2. Choose the current interest rate on the chart above. Then multiply the number of 1000s in the amount to be financed by the dollar amount corresponding with the current interest rate.

96.00	*number of $1000s in mortgage*
x $6.66	*rate/$1000 at 7% interest*
$639.36	*monthly mortgage rate*

How do you think you would find out what the current interest rates are for home mortgages? Write your ideas here:

_____

_____

_____

Your Mortgage Payment

Now complete your own calculations for a mortgage payment on a 30-year loan. Follow the method shown on the previous page for the condominium and house you have chosen.

	Condo	House

Finding Your Down Payment

Enter the price of your desired housing here (A). $ _____ (A) $ _____ (A)

Multiply that figure by the required
down payment. Let's say 10%. **X** .10   **X** .10

This is your required down payment (B). $ _____ (B) $ _____ (B)

It is the amount you must save before you purchase.

Finding the Amount Needed to Be Financed

Subtract your down payment (B) from your $ _____ (A) $ _____ (A)
cost of housing (A) $ – _____ (B) $ – _____ (B)

    (A) – (B) = (C)

(C) is the amount to be financed $ _____ (C) $ _____ (C)

Finding Your Monthly Mortgage Payments

Divide the amount to be financed by 1000.

    (C) ÷ 1000 = (D) _____ (D)   _____ (D)

From the chart on page 19 locate the rate of
interest your local bank would currently charge you
for a 30-year fixed rate mortgage. Your instructor can give
you an idea of what the current interest rate is.
(*Round to the nearest whole number.*)

What is the current interest rate for 30-year _____ % (E)   _____ % (E)
fixed rate mortgages?

Locate the dollar amount next to that rate (E)
on the chart, page 19. $ _____ (F) $ _____ (F)

Now multiply the number of thousands in **X** _____ (D)   **X** _____ (D)
the amount you want to finance (D) by (F).

    (D) X (F) = Monthly mortgage payment

Monthly mortgage payment $ _____ $ _____

**Enter the monthly mortgage payment for your condo (column C)
and your house (column D) on page 17.**

Property Taxes (Columns C and D, line 2)

You will need to calculate property taxes for property you already own. (As a renter you do not pay property taxes directly. However, your landlord does, so this is already factored into your monthly rent.)

Your research: Some states calculate property taxes by a certain percentage. Find out what the percentage is for calculating property taxes in your area and enter that figure here: _____

How is that figure expressed as a decimal? _____ (G)

Formula

> To find your annual property tax you must multiply the value (cost) of the house/condo by the percentage used to figure property tax.

Example:

Using an average figure: To illustrate this problem, let's say property taxes are 2% of the value of the condo. To calculate property taxes, multiply the price of the condo by 2% (.02).

For example, a condominium priced at $120,000 multiplied by 2% (.02) results in property taxes of $2,400.00 per year.

$120,000	*value of condo*
x .02	*property tax percentage*
$2,400	*annual property tax*

The **monthly** taxes are calculated by dividing $2,400.00 by 12 for an amount of $200.00.

$ 200.00	*monthly property tax*
12 ⟌ $2,400.00	*annual property tax*

Now find the estimated property tax for the properties you've chosen.

	C Condo	D House
Cost of the property	$ _____	$ _____
Times the percentage of property tax (G)	**X**_____	**X**_____
Annual property tax	$ _____	$ _____
Monthly property tax	$ _____	$ _____

Enter the appropriate property tax amount in columns C and D, line 2 of your BUDGET WORKSHEET on page 17.

✖ ➗

Insurance (All Columns, line 3)

You will need to have property insurance if you have a mortgage or loan on property you own.

Your research: Call an insurance agent or bank loan officer, describe the properties you are researching and ask them to quote the monthly insurance costs per month. Enter those figures on line 3 of your chart on page 17.

Example:

> **Using an average figure:** For housing insurance, multiply the home price by .25% (.0025 or one quarter of one percent). For example, the home price of $96,000 multiplied by .25% results in annual insurance costs of $240. The monthly insurance is calculated by dividing $240 by 12 for an amount of $20.00. Enter the appropriate insurance amount in line 3 of your chart on page 17.

$96,000	*value of condo*	$ 20.00	*monthly insurance cost*
x .0025	*average insurance percentage*	12 ⟌ $240.00	
$240.00	*annual insurance cost*		

Now, using your figures from page 16, find the monthly insurance costs for your condo and house.

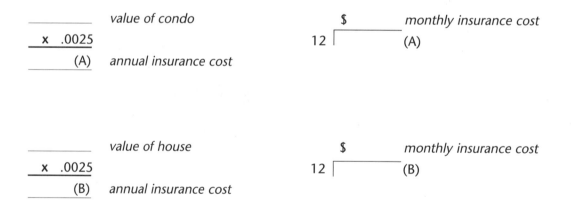

_____	*value of condo*	$ _____	*monthly insurance cost*
x .0025		12 ⟌ _____	(A)
_____ (A)	*annual insurance cost*		

_____	*value of house*	$ _____	*monthly insurance cost*
x .0025		12 ⟌ _____	(B)
_____ (B)	*annual insurance cost*		

Homeowner's Association Fees (Column C, line 4 only)

For this exercise, assume that only condominiums have homeowner's association fees.

Your Research: Call the classified ad number for the condo you chose and ask for the homeowner's association fee.

> **If using an average figure:** Use the figure of $100 per month.

CareerChoices.com

Utilities (All columns, line 5)

Sometimes utilities are included in the monthly rental fee for rental properties. Review your classified advertisement to decide if this is the case.

Your research: Determine the approximate square footage of each housing unit. Then call your local utility companies (gas, electric, water, etc.) and ask what an estimated average bill would be for each unit. Enter these figures on your MONTHLY HOUSING BUDGET WORKSHEET for each housing type.

You can ask friends or family members who have dwellings similar in size to the ones you chose to estimate their average monthly utility bills.

Using an average figure: Use the following figures for a 3 bedroom house/apartment. These figures assume you will be conservative with your resources.

Example:

Gas & Electric $100, Water $25, Trash Disposal $12, Cable TV $30.

	A Rent Apartment	B Rent House	C Own Condo	D Own House
Gas & Electric	_____	_____	_____	_____
Water	_____	_____	_____	_____
Trash Disposal	_____	_____	_____	_____
Cable T.V.	_____	_____	_____	_____
Total Utilities	_____	_____	_____	_____

Enter the total utility costs for each type of housing on page 17, line 1.4.

Telephone (All Columns, line 6)

Your research: Decide how many long distance phone calls you will make each month, to whom, and for how long. Will you make your calls during the early morning or during late evening to save money?

Ask to see copies of your parents' or friend's phone bills so you can better estimate your monthly phone costs. Add long-distance charges to the monthly standard rate.

Monthly standard rate (first phone)	_____
Monthly standard rate (additional phone)	_____
Projected long-distance charges	_____
Special services (i.e., Call Waiting)	_____
Total	_____

Enter on page 17, line 1.5 in each column.

Using an average figure: Assume that your monthly telephone bill will be $40. This figure is based on 2 or 3 fifteen-minute long-distance calls per week using a low-cost long-distance provider. You'll need to shop carefully. Did you know there are websites that provide comparisons between long distance providers? How would you find these websites?

What's Your Choice

Using the information you've gathered on the preceding eight pages, complete the MONTHLY HOUSING BUDGET WORKSHEET on page 17. Total your costs for each type of housing, decide which is most appealing to you, and place those housing figures on your Budget Profile on pages 13, line items 1.1 to 1.5.

Explain here why you chose what you did.

_____

_____

_____

Was your decision based more on a rational, logical reason (how the numbers worked for you) or an emotional reason (how you felt about your choice)?

_____

_____

If Renting is Your Choice . . . How Much will it Cost to Move In?

You've decided to rent an apartment or house. The following are the initial costs to be budgeted when moving into rental housing.

Formula for Costs of Moving into Rental Property:

First Month's Rent + Last Month's Rent + Cleaning Deposit + Security Deposit = Total Move in Cost

As you read the classified advertisements in your local newspaper under "Rentals," look for specific requirements like "first, last and cleaning deposit required." If these are not included you should inquire whether a cleaning deposit and the last month's rent are required.

For your budget, assume the cleaning deposit is equal to one month's rent.

The security deposit is usually 50% of one month's rent and therefore the formula for figuring it is:

$$\frac{\text{monthly rent} \times .50}{\text{security deposit}}$$

How much will it cost to move into the apartment you chose in column A on page 17 on your MONTHLY HOUSING BUDGET WORKSHEET? Show you work below:

First Month's Rent + _____

Last Month's Rent + _____

Cleaning Deposit + _____

Security Deposit + _____ *(50% of monthly rent)*

Total Costs of Moving In _____

How much would it cost to move into the rental house described in column B on page 17? Show your work below:

First Month's Rent + _____

Last Month's Rent + _____

Cleaning Deposit + _____

Security Deposit + _____ *(50% of monthly rent)*

Total Costs of Moving In _____

Form a group with 3 to 5 classmates and give your mind a workout. Use the brainpower of the combined group to try to answer these advanced math problems. Brainstorm possible answers to the following questions. Together you will be able to come up with the solutions.

How Numbers Can Help You Make the Best Choices

Study the chart on page 79 of *Career Choices* entitled HOME AFFORDABILITY, CITY BY CITY.

1. What do you think the Home Affordability Ratio represents?

2. Would it be easier to afford a home in Louisville, Kentucky, or in Los Angeles, California, based on the data presented in this chart? Why?

3. What is the mathematical formula for figuring the Home Affordability Ratio? Analyze the chart and you can probably figure it out. Write the formula here.

4. Imagine you have been offered two jobs, one as head custodian for a high school in Topeka, KS paying $25,500 per year, and the other as a senior maintenance worker in an office building in Portland, OR paying $31,300 per year. Owning you own home is important to you and your family. With that in mind, which job makes the most sense? Consult the Home Affordability chart on page 79 of *Career Choices*.

    a. If the median home price in Topeka is $124,475, what is the home affordability ratio of the custodian job?

    b. If the median home price in Portland is $275,725, what is the home affordability ratio of the maintenance job?

    c. Which job would you choose and for what reasons?

Home Affordability Across the Country

Prices of homes can vary greatly from one city to another.

As you decide where you want to live, it is helpful to be able to compare the cost of housing to the area where you currently live.

The following index, developed by Coldwell Banker Realtors, can be helpful. Moving to an expensive area can sharply cut your standard of living, even if you get a big raise. On the other hand, if you can't afford a home where you now live, by moving to an area where houses are less expensive (a city with a lower index), you may be able to afford to be a home owner.

The figures on the following chart are the 2005 average prices for a typical 2,200 square-foot home, with four bedrooms, 2½ bathrooms, a family room and a two-car garage. The city affordability index is factored for cities across the country.

If you want to investigate what your house (page 17) would cost in other parts of the country, use the following formula.

$$\left(\text{Value of the house you chose} \div \text{Your city's index}\right) \times \text{The index of the city you'd like to investigate} = \text{The cost of buying a similar home in that new city}$$

State/Area	Market	'05 price	Index
Alabama	Huntsville	$188,466	53
	Mobile	$180,575	51
Alaska	Anchorage	$248,491	70
	Juneau	$420,537	119
Arizona	Flagstaff	$326,700	92
	Mesa	$214,300	60
	Phoenix	$266,667	75
	Scottsdale	$376,300	106
	Tucson	$212,600	60
Arkansas	Fayetteville	$207,325	59
	Fort Smith	$164,125	46
	Little Rock	$166,800	47
California	Bakersfield	$313,750	89
	Fremont	$786,500	222
	Fresno	$305,000	86
	Grass Valley	$361,250	102
	Modesto	$340,333	96
	Monterey Peninsula	$736,000	208
	Oakland/Montclair	$955,000	269
	Pleasanton	$771,000	218
	Sacramento	$348,600	98
	San Francisco	$1,125,500	318
	San Jose	$952,500	269
	San Mateo	$1,142,500	322
	San Rafael	$739,667	209
	Thousand Oaks	$671,433	189
	Walnut Creek	$711,750	201
Los Angeles Area	Beverly Hills	$1,313,750	371
	Long Beach	$835,500	236
	Palos Verdes	$980,000	277
	Pasadena	$714,500	202
	Mission Viejo	$756,300	213
	Newport Beach	$1,174,375	331
	Santa Clarita	$497,725	140
	Riverside/Ontario	$360,050	102
San Diego Area	Encinitas	$700,000	198
	La Jolla	$1,708,333	482
	Palm Desert	$398,350	112
	San Diego	$607,475	171
Colorado	Colorado Springs	$180,666	51
	Denver	$249,333	70
	Fort Collins	$264,966	75
Connecticut	Danbury	$365,775	103
	Greenwich	$1,192,500	337
	Litchfield County/ Torrington	$220,000	62
	Naugatuck	$333,675	94
	New Canaan	$1,081,038	305
	Norwalk	$548,000	155
	Ridgefield	$666,600	188
	Stamford	$681,125	192
	Westport	$753,000	212
Delaware	Wilmington	$348,200	98
Florida	Boca Raton	$304,333	86
	Clearwater/ St. Petersburg	$310,613	88
	Ft. Lauderdale/ Coral Springs	$323,750	91
	Jacksonville	$267,106	75
	Ft. Myers	$274,167	77
	Miami/Coral Gables	$507,225	143
	Naples	$346,667	98
	Orlando	$244,730	69
	Sarasota	$279,510	79

State/Area	Market	'05 price	Index
Florida (continued)	Tallahassee	$245,725	69
	Tampa	$247,375	70
	West Palm Beach	$323,975	91
Georgia	Athens	$221,300	62
	Atlanta	$283,900	80
	Dalton	$172,725	49
	Savannah	$239,625	68
Hawaii	Honolulu	$614,750	173
	Kehei, Maui	$591,630	167
Idaho	Boise	$192,740	54
Illinois	Aurora	$275,967	78
	Barrington	$530,125	150
	Bloomington	$206,525	58
	Carol Stream	$333,667	94
	Champaign	$218,966	62
	Chicago	$763,333	215
	Deerfield	$510,750	144
	Elgin	$257,167	73
	Flossmoor	$272,000	77
	Joliet	$225,366	64
	Naperville	$322,000	91
	Orland Park	$308,500	87
	Peoria	$203,666	57
	Rockford	$179,250	51
	Springfield	$168,800	48
Indiana	Evansville	$166,565	47
	Fort Wayne	$183,625	52
	Indianapolis	$189,488	53
	Munster	$299,666	85
	South Bend	$171,850	48
	Valpariso	$222,500	63
Iowa	Cedar Rapids	$187,650	53
	Des Moines	$242,400	68
	Dubuque	$177,725	50
	Sioux City	$227,875	64
Kansas	Lawrence	$226,800	64
	Overland Park	$206,802	58
	Leavenworth/ Lansing	$189,025	53
	Topeka/ Shawnee County	$141,850	40
	Wichita/ Sedgwick County	$154,337	44
Kentucky	Lexington	$155,983	44
	Louisville	$223,518	63
Louisiana	Baton Rouge	$197,057	56
	Lafayette	$171,750	48
	New Orleans	$250,375	71
	Shreveport/ Bossier City	$214,475	61
Maine	Augusta	$195,000	55
	Bangor	$213,400	60
	Portland	$334,800	94
Maryland	Annapolis/ Anne Arundel County	$337,950	95
	Metro Baltimore	$293,687	83
	Columbia/ Howard County	$391,833	111
	Bethesda/ Chevy Chase/ Montgomery County	$491,440	139
Massachusetts	Acton	$700,000	198
	Boston	$1,053,594	297
	Framingham	$509,966	144

State/Area	Market	'05 price	Index	State/Area	Market	'05 price	Index
Massachusetts (continued)	Wellesley	$1,102,500	311	North Carolina (continued)	Greensboro	$178,500	50
	Barnstable/Cape Cod	$548,500	155		Raleigh	$218,307	62
	Greater Springfield	$291,666	82		Winston-Salem	$190,833	54
	Worcester	$311,966	88	North Dakota	Fargo	$184,262	52
	Lexington	$715,000	202	Ohio	Akron	$176,000	50
Michigan	Greater Lansing	$240,475	68		Canton	$184,633	52
	Grand Rapids	$199,700	56		Cincinnati	$234,167	66
	Jackson	$236,150	67		Columbus	$231,225	65
	Midland/				Dayton	$166,600	47
	Saginaw/Bay City	$219,500	62		Greater Cleveland	$217,666	61
	Traverse City	$229,967	65		Toledo	$180,333	51
Detroit Area	Ann Arbor	$340,000	96	Oklahoma	Oklahoma City	$182,158	51
	Detroit Metro	$282,480	80		Tulsa	$138,250	39
	Port Huron	$219,534	62	Oregon	Eugene	$265,250	75
	Auburn Hills/				Portland	$262,600	74
	Lake Orion	$260,166	73		Salem	$225,633	64
Minnesota	Minneapolis	$354,175	100	Pennsylvania	Allentown	$304,500	86
	St. Cloud	$229,433	65		Harrisburg	$228,044	64
	Rochester	$208,847	59		Philadelphia County/		
	St. Paul	$346,663	98		Center City		
Mississippi	Gulfport/Biloxi	$166,333	47		Philadelphia	$488,675	138
	Jackson	$219,875	62		Pittsburgh	$243,125	69
	Tupelo	$166,225	47		York	$239,840	68
Missouri	Kansas City	$201,600	57	Rhode Island	Providence	$440,000	124
	St. Louis	$229,325	65	South Carolina	Charleston	$290,000	82
	Springfield	$159,933	45		Columbia	$175,500	50
Montana	Kalispell	$159,684	45		Greenville	$185,125	52
	Helena	$158,100	45	South Dakota	Rapid City	$174,700	49
Nebraska	Omaha	$169,900	48		Sioux Falls	$164,875	47
Nevada	Las Vegas	$263,125	74	Tennessee	Chattanooga	$180,425	51
	Reno/Sparks	$347,100	98		Knoxville	$145,696	41
New Hampshire	Amherst	$296,625	84		Memphis	$176,125	50
	Portsmouth	$277,000	78		Nashville	$198,000	56
New Jersey	Atlantic County/			Texas	Amarillo	$174,300	49
	Absecon	$299,500	85		Corpus Christi	$168,700	48
	Camden County/				Austin	$202,628	57
	Cherry Hill	$257,883	73		Dallas	$236,313	67
	Basking Ridge	$603,375	170		El Paso	$174,667	49
	Clinton	$514,666	145		Fort Worth	$148,500	42
	Edison/Metuchen	$421,750	119		Houston	$173,512	49
	Gloucester County/				Killeen	$136,750	39
	Turnersville	$231,467	65		Lubbock	$166,875	47
	Madison	$603,333	170		Plano	$182,900	52
	Manalapan/Marlboro	$461,750	130		San Antonio	$205,125	58
	Montclair	$583,000	165	Utah	Salt Lake City	$238,288	67
	Ocean County/				Provo	$207,440	59
	Toms River	$332, 881	94	Vermont	Montpelier	$241,500	68
	Princeton Junction	$559,759	158	Virginia	Norfolk/Virginia Beach	$223,616	63
	Ridgewood	$752,500	212		Roanoke/Blacksburg	$206,487	58
	Sparta	$521,180	147		Richmond	$244,633	69
	Wayne	$501,950	142	Washington	Bellevue	$491,666	139
	Westfield	$672,450	190		Seattle	$341,333	96
New Mexico	Albuquerque	$228,452	64		Spokane	$207,321	59
New York	Albany	$258,301	73		Tacoma	$255,250	72
	Binghamton	$147,525	42		Tri-Cities	$225,125	64
	Buffalo	$228,000	64	West Virginia	Charleston	$195,667	55
	Orange County	$338,467	96	Wisconsin	Fox Cities	$249,200	70
	Queens/Bayside	$641,125	181		Green Bay	$263,200	74
	Rochester/SE sub.	$251,666	71		Madison	$248,248	70
	Staten Island	$520,000	147		Eau Claire	$151,433	43
	Syracuse	$205,350	58		Milwaukee	$310,000	87
	Yorktown Heights	$451,233	127	Wyoming	Cheyenne	$194,225	55
North Carolina	Charlotte	$190,625	54				
	Fayetteville	$183,267	52				

Where Do You Want to Live?

To compare the cost of a home where you currently live with the costs of other areas in the United States, you first need to know:

Price of the home you chose (see page 16): $_____

Index of your city or one similar to yours: _____
(Refer to pages 28 and 29.)

Your Ideal Location

Choose a city that intrigues you, one where you might like to live. Compare the cost of your chosen home with a similar home in that interesting city by working through the formula on page 27. Which area is more expensive?

Name of the ideal city: _____   Index for the ideal city: _____

Cost of a similar home in your ideal city $_____

An Affordable Location

You and your spouse want to own a home. You have just finished college and when you look at the expense of ownership in your home town, you realize you may have a better lifestyle if you move to another city or state. So before you begin job hunting, you study the index list, choose an area with a lower index than the one where you are currently living (yet still holds appeal to you) and compare the affordability.

More affordable city: _____   Index for the affordable city: _____

Cost of a similar home in the more affordable city: $_____

Affording Home Ownership on One Income

You and your spouse want to have a family and decide it is important for one of you to be home while your children are young. Therefore you decide to design a lifestyle that can be supported by one income. This will probably necessitate living in a part of the country where the cost of housing is most reasonable. From the index list on pages 28 and 29 choose the ten most affordable cities in America.

	City	State	Index
1.			
2.			
3.			
4.			
5.			
6.			
7.			
8.			
9.			
10.			

Star two of the above cities that you find interesting. How could you learn more about these cities?

Besides raising a family on one income, what would be other reasons you would choose to move to a more affordable city? List below.

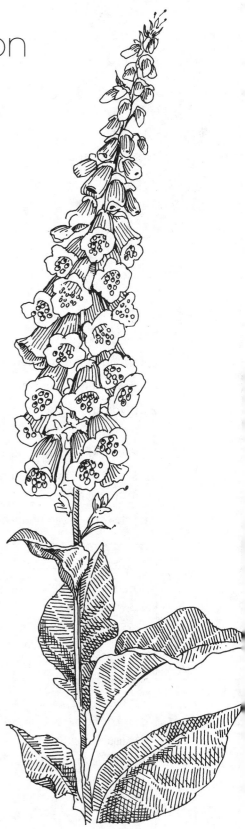

Transportation – Buying a Car

Read pages 80 and 81 in *Career Choices*.

What kind of transportation mode(s) do you plan to use when you are 29 years old?

_____ _____ _____

If you plan to own a car, describe it below:

What make _____ Model _____ Year _____

(Assume the same cars will be available as the ones we have on the market today.)

How many miles per month do you plan to drive? _____

Buying a Car

Before buying a car, you will need to answer these questions:

1. How much money will you need if you paid cash for the car described above?

2. If you are not able to pay cash to purchase a car, what is the amount of money you will need for a down payment?

3. What will your monthly payments be on a 48-month loan for the unpaid balance?

4. How much in interest charges will be added to the cost of the car if you decide to finance it?

An interest table to finance a car for 48 months might look like this:

Monthly Payments on 48-Month Car Loan										
Amt. of Loan	14%	13%	12%	11%	10%	9%	8%	7%	6%	5%
$5,000	$136.63	$134.14	$131.67	$129.23	$126.81	$124.43	$122.06	$119.73	$117.43	$115.15
$6,000	$163.96	$160.96	$158.00	$155.07	$152.18	$149.31	$146.48	$143.68	$140.91	$138.18
$7,000	$191.29	$187.79	$184.34	$180.82	$177.54	$174.20	$170.89	$167.62	$164.40	$161.21
$8,000	$218.61	$214.62	$210.67	$206.76	$202.90	$199.08	$195.30	$191.57	$187.88	$184.23
$9,000	$245.94	$241.45	$237.00	$232.61	$228.26	$223.79	$219.72	$215.52	$211.37	$207.26
$10,000	$273.26	$268.27	$263.34	$258.46	$253.63	$248.85	$244.13	$239.46	$234.85	$230.29
$11,000	$300.59	$295.10	$289.67	$284.30	$278.99	$273.74	$268.54	$263.41	$258.34	$253.32
$12,000	$327.92	$321.93	$310.01	$310.15	$304.35	$298.62	$292.95	$287.35	$281.82	$276.35
$13,000	$355.24	$348.76	$342.34	$335.99	$329.71	$323.51	$317.37	$311.30	$305.31	$299.38
$14,000	$382.57	$375.58	$368.67	$361.84	$355.08	$348.39	$341.78	$335.25	$328.79	$322.41
$15,000	$409.90	$402.41	$395.01	$387.68	$380.44	$373.28	$366.19	$359.19	$352.28	$345.44
$16,000	$437.22	$429.24	$421.34	$413.53	$405.80	$398.16	$390.61	$383.14	$375.76	$368.47
$17,000	$464.55	$456.07	$447.68	$439.37	$431.16	$423.05	$415.02	$407.09	$399.25	$391.50
$18,000	$491.98	$482.89	$474.01	$465.22	$456.53	$447.93	$439.43	$431.03	$422.73	$414.53
$19,000	$519.20	$509.72	$500.34	$491.06	$481.89	$472.82	$463.85	$454.98	$446.22	$437.56
$20,000	$546.53	$536.55	$526.68	$516.91	$507.25	$497.70	$488.26	$478.92	$469.70	$460.59

Example:

Let's say you bought a six-year-old mid-size coupe for $8,000. You were able to make a $1,000 down payment. Therefore, the unpaid balance that you must finance is $7,000. This is factored as follows:

$$\begin{array}{ll} \$8,000 & \textit{price of car} \\ -\ 1,000 & \textit{down payment} \\ \hline \$7,000 & \textit{unpaid balance} \end{array}$$

For this example let's say the interest rate charged to borrow money for a used car is 9%. By using the Interest Table, you'll find your monthly payment will be $174.20.

Now it is your turn to complete an exercise using the automobile you described on the preceding page.

Select a car you wish to buy and research the cost of that car in the classified ads. Assume for this exercise that you have saved $2,000 for the down payment. Plan your monthly car payments using the chart on page 32. Round the price to the nearest $1,000. Complete the following exercise worksheet.

Planning Your Monthly Car Payments

Make/Model/Year of Car _____ _____ _____

Price of Car $_____

Minus Down Payment – $2,000

= Unpaid Balance to Finance $_____

Select an interest rate from the chart that closely reflects the interest charged in your area for auto loans. You can find this figure by looking in the automobile advertisements in your newspaper or by calling a local bank. Look up the closest interest rate on the chart and find the monthly payment that most closely reflects your situation.

Interest Rate on a 48-month Loan _____%

Monthly Car Payment $_____

Enter the monthly car payment on page 13, line 2.1 of Your Budget Profile.

Trade-In Time?

Let's use this information another way.

The family car is starting to cost more to maintain than it's worth. Time to start thinking about a replacement. You sit down and, after reviewing your expenses and income, calculate that you can comfortably afford payments of $220 per month.

With $1,000 to put down on the replacement car, a trade-in allowance of $1,500 on your old car, and interest rates for a 48-month loan at 8%, what is the maximum you can spend for your car?

$ _____

Using the newspaper, choose at least one car that matches your financial constraints and describe it here.

Car

   Make/Model/Year of Car

_____ _____ _____   Price _____

   Mileage on odometer _____ Miles per gallon _____   Condition _____

Planning Monthly Gasoline Costs

Formulas:

To learn the number of gallons of gasoline used, divide the number of miles driven in a specific period by the average number of miles per gallon for your car.

To find the cost of gasoline required, multiply the cost of a gallon of gas by the number of gallons used.

Example:

Assume that gasoline costs $2.25 per gallon and your car gets 20 miles to the gallon. If each week you travel an average of 200 miles, you will use an average of 10 gallons of gasoline per week.

The calculation of your monthly gasoline cost is as follows:

A. Miles you plan to drive each week = 200 miles | 200 miles

B. Miles per gallon for your car = 20 miles per gallon | ÷ 20 miles per gallon

C. Gallons of gasoline per week = 10 gallons per week | 10 gallons per week
   This calculation is A divided by B

D. Cost per gallon of gasoline = $2.25 | $2.25 cost per gallon

E. Total cost of gasoline per week = $22.50 | $22.50 cost gasoline per week
   This calculation is C x D

F. Multiply by 4 weeks per month (x 4) | **X** 4

G. Gasoline expense per month = $90.00 | $90.00 cost of gasoline per month
   This calculation is E x 4

* This was an average price of a gallon of gasoline at the time this book was printed. Prices can be seasonal and vary not only from state to state but city to city. Note the prices on the signs outside the gas stations in your area.

Your Calculations of Gasoline Cost Per Month

In order to calculate your monthly gasoline cost, it is necessary to know how many miles per gallon the car you may purchase will get. (Use the same car you listed on page 33.)

You also need to estimate the number of miles per week you are likely to drive. (For example, how far will you live from work? How many errands will you run? Do your friends and family live in another town?) With that information in mind, complete the following calculations:

A. Miles you plan to drive per week   _____ miles

B. Miles per gallon for your car   ÷ _____ miles per gallon

C. Gallons of gasoline per week   _____ gallons per week
   This calculation is A divided by B

D. Cost per gallon of gasoline $_____ cost per gallon
   $1.40 average or research gas costs in your area

E. Total cost of gasoline per week $_____ gasoline cost per week
   This calculation is C x D

F. Multiply by 4 weeks per month   **X** 4

G. Gasoline expense per month $_____ gasoline cost per month
   This calculation is E x 4

Enter your monthly gas cost on page 13, line 2.2 of Your Budget Profile.

Extra Credit — Going that Extra Mile in Your Calculations

How Much Extra will it Cost You to Finance Your Car?

If you can't pay cash for your car, how much extra will it cost to finance your car over four years? This is usually a hidden cost of a car, something the sales people don't talk about. However, it costs **real dollars** and is an important calculation for you to make when deciding how much you want to pay for a car. The following formula will help in your decision making.

In this example, over a four-year (48-month) period, the interest cost is $1,361.60 for the privilege of borrowing money. The calculation of the interest cost is as follows:

Monthly payment on a $7,000 loan at 9% is $174.20 *(see the chart on page 32)*.

Multiply $174.20 by 48 months and you find your total amount repaid is $8,361.60.
($174.20 x 48 = $8,361.60)

Now subtract the loan amount of $7,000 from $8,361.60.

The interest charges for the 48-month loan = $1,361.60.

Complete the following for your chosen car from page 32:

A. The unpaid balance to be financed
   (Cost of car minus the down payment)

$ _____ (A)

B. Monthly interest rate
   (Get this figure from the newspaper or online)

_____ % (B)

C. Monthly payment for that interest rate
   (Look this up on the chart on page 32)

$ _____ (C)

x 48 months

D. The monthly payment **times** 48 months = The total amount to be paid on the loan.

(C X 48 = D)

$ _____ (D)

E. The total amount to be paid on the loan **minus** the unpaid balance to be financed = Total interest charges for 48 months

– $ _____ (A)

(D – A = E)

Total interest charges for 48 months

$ _____ (E)

How much will it actually cost you to purchase your car if you use credit? *(Hint: Remember to add back in your down payment to the total amount to be paid on the loan.)*

$ _____

Group Think — Extra Extra Credit

With a group of 3 to 5 of your classmates, try to figure out this problem.

PROBLEM   For the last four years you have saved $125 per month, which is in a bank savings account earning 3% interest. You need a car and have found a used compact car (in good condition) that will cost exactly what you have in your savings account.

1. If you put ⅓ of your savings down and finance the rest for four years at 10%, estimate your monthly payments? (Use chart on page 32.)

2. How much will you pay in interest over four years?

3. If you take your money out of your bank account to pay for the car, how much will you **actually** save in interest? Remember to factor in the interest you would have earned on your savings account.

4. Which would you decide to do? Pay cash for the car from your savings? Finance the car? Explain why you made your choice.

5. Are there any other choices or strategies for paying for or financing your car? (Be creative and keep it legal!)

Transportation Insurance and Maintenance

Basic car insurance is called "Bodily Injury and Property Damage Insurance." This covers the owner's liability for injury inflicted on other persons. Additional insurance you can carry is called "Collision and Comprehensive Insurance" which covers the cost of repairs or replacement of the vehicle.

An insurance agent calculates insurance costs based on four factors:

1. The area where the car is frequently driven

2. Purpose for which the car is used

3. Age of the driver

4. The driving history of the driver (tickets, accidents, etc.) to be insured.

Call an automobile insurance agent and get an estimate of what it would cost you each year to insure the car you have chosen.

$_____(A) yearly insurance

Divide that amount by 12 to come up with the monthly cost.
$$\frac{\$\text{_____}(A)}{12} =$$

Ask a mechanic to help you figure the annual yearly maintenance costs of the car you have chosen. A lot will depend upon the condition of the car. Is it new and still under warranty? Is it older and in need of repairs or tires, etc.? Use the figure that the mechanic and you decide on. To find out your monthly requirements, divide that number by 12.

$_____(A) Monthly maintenance budget

Using an average figure

Using the chart at the bottom of page 81 of *Career Choices,* assume that car maintenance costs are as follows:

Maintenance and tires	$ .059 per mile	*(5.9¢/mile)*
Insurance	$ .01 per mile	*(1¢/mile)*
Total	$ .069 per mile	*(6.9¢/mile)*

Using the costs above, complete the following:

A. Weekly number of miles you drive

_____ (A)

X 4 weeks per month

B. Monthly miles
   (weekly miles x 4)

_____ (B)

C. Maintenance and insurance cost per mile = $.069
   *(found on page 81 of **Career Choices**)*

X $ .069   (C)

D. Total monthly cost of maintenance and insurance
   This calculation is B x C

_____ (D)

Choose one set of figures from either your own research or using an average figure and enter this amount on page 13, line 2.3 of Your Budget Profile.

Public Transportation

Do you plan to use public transportation occasionally or exclusively?

If you don't know the cost of a bus ride in your community, assume that a one-way bus ticket costs $1.25. Complete the following chart:

A. One-way bus ticket price $\qquad$ \$_____(A)

B. Number of bus trips you estimate
   you will take per week **X**_____(B)

C. Bus transportation cost per week _____(C)
   This calculation is A x B

X 4   weeks per month

D. Monthly bus transportation costs _____(D)
   C x 4 = D

If you intend to use public transportation, enter the total monthly public transportation cost on page 13, line 2.4 of Your Budget Profile.

Case Study

Form a group of 3 to 5 classmates to work through this problem.

You are married and both you and your spouse work at the same place, which is 15 miles away. Your starting times each day are different so you cannot travel to work together. You are saving for the down payment on a house.

Sitting down with pencil and paper, you need to decide if it makes more sense for you to purchase a second car or for one of you to ride the bus each day.

First you list all the facts in the problem.

1. Your work site is 15 miles away. You both work 5 days per week, Monday through Friday.

2. The car you have chosen, a 1993 compact car, gets 30 miles to a gallon.

3. Gasoline costs $1.40 per gallon.

4. A bus ticket is $1.25 each way.

5. The used car you would purchase would have monthly payments of $76.10 per month because you would borrow $3000 at 10% interest. Your uncle will give you as a belated wedding present the $1000 down payment if you decide to purchase this car.

6. The maintenance costs would average $.031/mile.

7. The minimal insurance cost would be $360 per year.

8. You would only use the second car to get back and forth to work.

How much would you spend monthly on public transportation? $ _____

How much would you spend monthly on a second car? $ _____

Will you buy a car or continue to take public transportation? Why? Convice your classmates of the soundness of your group's decision.

Yearly Clothing Budget

Read and complete the exercises on page 82 of *Career Choices.*

Using the following worksheets, plan an annual clothing budget for yourself and the dependents you listed on page 12. Once you have found the annual budget for each member of your proposed family, enter those figures on page 13 of Your Budget Profile.

The following chart is an example of the costs of items you may want to include in your budget. You may use these figures as an average or research your own.

Morgan's Clothes

Item	Unit Costs
Blouse	$18.00 to $36.00
Shirt	$14.00 to $22.00
Dress	$40.00 to $75.00
Skirt	$40.00
Jacket	$45.00
Long Coat	$85.00
Dress Slacks	$32.00 to 46.00
Pants	$35.00
Suit	$85.00 to $185.00
Underwear	3 pair for $20.00
Bra	$20.00
Socks	3 pair for $12.00
Hose	$3.00
T-shirt	3 for $15.00
Shoes	$40.00 to $70.00

Items to consider when planning your annual clothing budget:

- ✓ Work/School outfits
- ✓ Dress-up clothes
- ✓ Underclothes
- ✓ Shoes
- ✓ Socks/Hose
- ✓ Outer wear — Jackets, Long coats, Sweaters
- ✓ Recreational clothes
- ✓ Accessories

Hints:

Under "other items" you might include such things as swimwear, special work clothes (depending on what you visualize your future to be), exercise or recreational wear, religious clothing, etc.

Think of ways you can save money. It's great fun to find a bargain! Shopping on sale or shopping at the local consignment shop is a way to stretch your clothing dollar. Some people sew their own clothes.

Your Annual Clothing Budget

Formula for determining Your Annual Clothing Budget:

STEP 1: First list all the types of clothing you will need. (Column A)

STEP 2: Then estimate how many of each type of clothing you will need during the next year. (Column B)

STEP 3: Now estimate the average cost of one piece of that type of clothing. (Column C)

STEP 4: Multiply the average cost of a type of clothing with the number needed of that type to find the total annual cost/type. B X C = D

STEP 5: Finally total all annual costs/type to find out your total budget for clothing.

A Description	B Number of Items per Year		C Average Cost per Item		D Total Annual Cost/Type
Blouses	_____	X	$ _____	=	$ _____
Shirts	_____	X	$ _____	=	$ _____
Dresses	_____	X	$ _____	=	$ _____
Skirts	_____	X	$ _____	=	$ _____
Pants	_____	X	$ _____	=	$ _____
Dress Slacks	_____	X	$ _____	=	$ _____
Jackets	_____	X	$ _____	=	$ _____
Long Coats	_____	X	$ _____	=	$ _____
Suits	_____	X	$ _____	=	$ _____
Underwear	_____	X	$ _____	=	$ _____
Bras	_____	X	$ _____	=	$ _____
Socks	_____	X	$ _____	=	$ _____
Hose	_____	X	$ _____	=	$ _____
T-shirts	_____	X	$ _____	=	$ _____
Shoes	_____	X	$ _____	=	$ _____
Sleepwear	_____	X	$ _____	=	$ _____
Other (List) _____	_____	X	$ _____	=	$ _____
Other (List) _____	_____	X	$ _____	=	$ _____

Your Total Annual Clothing Budget $ _____

To find the monthly cost, divide your total annual clothing budget by 12.

$ _____ monthly clothing budget for yourself

Enter total on page 13, line 3.1 of Your Budget Profile.

Spouse Clothing Budget

A Description	B Number of Items per Year		C Average Cost per Item		D Total Annual Cost/Type
Blouses	_____	X	$ _____	=	$ _____
Shirts	_____	X	$ _____	=	$ _____
Dresses	_____	X	$ _____	=	$ _____
Skirts	_____	X	$ _____	=	$ _____
Pants	_____	X	$ _____	=	$ _____
Dress Slacks	_____	X	$ _____	=	$ _____
Jackets	_____	X	$ _____	=	$ _____
Long Coats	_____	X	$ _____	=	$ _____
Suits	_____	X	$ _____	=	$ _____
Underwear	_____	X	$ _____	=	$ _____
Bras	_____	X	$ _____	=	$ _____
Socks	_____	X	$ _____	=	$ _____
Hose	_____	X	$ _____	=	$ _____
T-shirts	_____	X	$ _____	=	$ _____
Shoes	_____	X	$ _____	=	$ _____
Sleepwear	_____	X	$ _____	=	$ _____
Other (List) _____	_____	X	$ _____	=	$ _____
Other (List) _____	_____	X	$ _____	=	$ _____
Other (List) _____	_____	X	$ _____	=	$ _____

Your Spouse's Total Annual Clothing Budget $ _____

To find the monthly cost, divide your spouses's total annual clothing budget by 12.

$ _____   monthly clothing budget for your spouse
12 ⌐

Enter total on page 13, line 3.2 of Your Budget Profile.

Worksheet for Children's Clothing Budget

CHILD'S AGE _____   GENDER _____

A Description	B Number of Pieces or Items per Year		C Average Cost Per Item		D Total Annual Cost per Type of Clothing
Cloth Diapers	_____	X	$ _____	=	$ _____
Disposable Diapers	_____	X	$ _____	=	$ _____
Bibs	_____	X	$ _____	=	$ _____
T-Shirts	_____	X	$ _____	=	$ _____
Underwear	_____	X	$ _____	=	$ _____
Bras	_____	X	$ _____	=	$ _____
Shorts	_____	X	$ _____	=	$ _____
Pants/Slacks	_____	X	$ _____	=	$ _____
Belts	_____	X	$ _____	=	$ _____
Socks	_____	X	$ _____	=	$ _____
Shoes	_____	X	$ _____	=	$ _____
Dresses	_____	X	$ _____	=	$ _____
Skirts	_____	X	$ _____	=	$ _____
Hats	_____	X	$ _____	=	$ _____
Jackets	_____	X	$ _____	=	$ _____
Sportcoats	_____	X	$ _____	=	$ _____
Sweaters	_____	X	$ _____	=	$ _____
Pantyhose	_____	X	$ _____	=	$ _____
Sleepwear	_____	X	$ _____	=	$ _____
Sportsclothes (Uniforms, etc.)	_____	X	$ _____	=	$ _____
Jewelry	_____	X	$ _____	=	$ _____
Other (List) _____	_____	X	$ _____	=	$ _____

Total Annual Clothing Budget for this Child $ _____

$ _____ monthly clothing budget allowance

12)‾$‾‾‾

⊕ ⊗ ÷

Worksheet for Children's Clothing Budget

CHILD'S AGE _____   GENDER _____

A Description	B Number of Pieces or Items per Year		C Average Cost Per Item		D Total Annual Cost per Type of Clothing
Cloth Diapers	_____	X	$ _____	=	$ _____
Disposable Diapers	_____	X	$ _____	=	$ _____
Bibs	_____	X	$ _____	=	$ _____
T-Shirts	_____	X	$ _____	=	$ _____
Underwear	_____	X	$ _____	=	$ _____
Bras	_____	X	$ _____	=	$ _____
Shorts	_____	X	$ _____	=	$ _____
Pants/Slacks	_____	X	$ _____	=	$ _____
Belts	_____	X	$ _____	=	$ _____
Socks	_____	X	$ _____	=	$ _____
Shoes	_____	X	$ _____	=	$ _____
Dresses	_____	X	$ _____	=	$ _____
Skirts	_____	X	$ _____	=	$ _____
Hats	_____	X	$ _____	=	$ _____
Jackets	_____	X	$ _____	=	$ _____
Sportcoats	_____	X	$ _____	=	$ _____
Sweaters	_____	X	$ _____	=	$ _____
Pantyhose	_____	X	$ _____	=	$ _____
Sleepwear	_____	X	$ _____	=	$ _____
Sportsclothes (Uniforms, etc.) _____		X	$ _____	=	$ _____
Jewelry	_____	X	$ _____	=	$ _____
Other (List) _____	_____	X	$ _____	=	$ _____

Total Annual Clothing Budget for this Child $ _____

$ _____   monthly clothing budget allowance

12 ⟌ $ _____

Add child(ren)'s monthly clothing allowance together and enter total on page 13, line 3.3 of Your Budget Profile.

Preparing a Food Budget

1. Read and answer the questions on page 84 of *Career Choices.*

2. Eating is one of the pleasures in life and with planning you can eat well on a budget. So we have paid extra attention to the *numbers as they relate to food.* Study the following pages on food groups, nutrition, food budgeting, substitutions for missing ingredients, and stretching your food dollar. Add your own ideas for additional ways to stretch your food dollar.

3. What do you like to eat? Plan for one week using the worksheet titled "Planning Your Weekly Meals." (page 53)

4. Review the "Sample Shopping List." The items on the list are grouped the way they are stocked in a grocery store. Planning a shopping list for the grocery store always helps you cut down on your grocery bill. Write your week's grocery list using the ingredients needed for your menus.

5. On the Weekly Grocery Costs worksheet (pages 56 and 57) list items you would buy for one week based on the family profile that you chose earlier on page 12 .

The worksheet is divided into two parts:

Part One: Produce, Bakery, Dairy Products and Canned Goods — These are items you need to buy each week. To get a monthly total cost, multiply your total cost by 4.

Part Two: Packaged goods, Household Products, and Sundries — These are items you buy less often. On your shopping list, show the quantity you might buy per month.

6. After you have completed your grocery costs worksheet on pages 56 and 57, review the list and add the codes given below that best describe the shopping pattern for each listed item.

S = Government Surplus — Least Expensive

T = Store's Own Label — Usually less expensive than brand names

B = Brand Label — Brand names as seen in advertisements

G = Gourmet Brand — Usually most expensive

In marking each item on your shopping list, if you plan to buy government surplus, mark an item with an **S**. If you plan to buy the store's own label, mark those items with a **T**. If you plan to buy a brand name, mark those items with a **B**, and if you plan to buy a gourmet brand, mark those items with a **G**.

7. Once you have gathered all the prices for your shopping list and totaled your costs, multiply your weekly expenses by 4 and get a monthly total. Now compare your estimated monthly grocery expenses to the chart on page 85 of *Career Choices*. How does your estimate compare with these various costs.

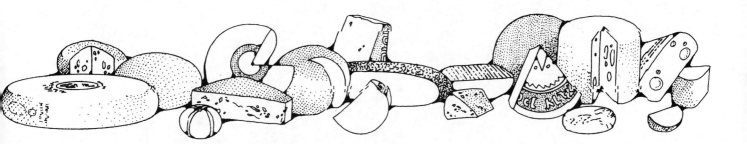

Learning about Nutrition and Shopping Can Save You Money!

Before you begin planning your menus, shopping lists and **food budget** it may be helpful to review some basic information on nutrition. Remember, **information is power**. If you become a conscientious consumer, it will save you thousands of dollars over your lifetime, while maintaining optimum health and vitality.

Food Pyramid — Their Contribution to Your Diet

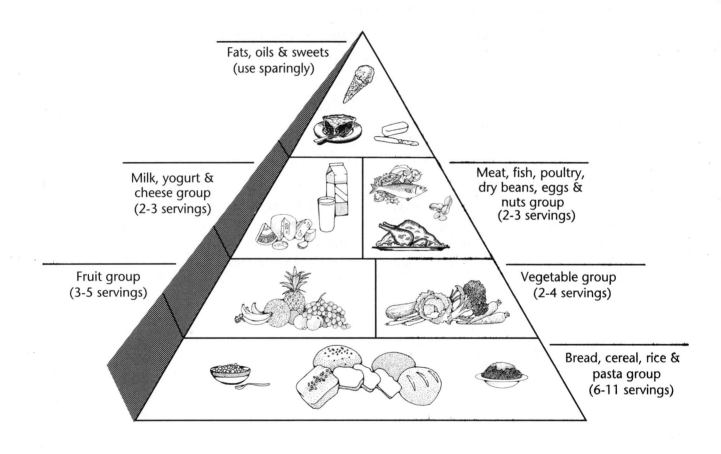

Fats, oils & sweets
(use sparingly)

Milk, yogurt &
cheese group
(2-3 servings)

Meat, fish, poultry,
dry beans, eggs &
nuts group
(2-3 servings)

Fruit group
(3-5 servings)

Vegetable group
(2-4 servings)

Bread, cereal, rice &
pasta group
(6-11 servings)

List five foods from each food group.

Bread, cereal, rice and pasta

_____

_____

_____

_____

_____

Vegetables

_____

_____

_____

_____

_____

Fruits

_____

_____

_____

_____

_____

Milk, yogurt and cheese

_____

_____

_____

_____

_____

Meat, fish, poultry, beans, eggs and nuts

_____

_____

_____

_____

_____

Fats, oils and sweets

_____

_____

_____

_____

_____

SOURCES OF VITAMIN A AND VITAMIN C			
Vitamin A		**Vitamin C**	
GOOD	FAIR	GOOD	FAIR
Apricots	Other dark green leaves	Broccoli	Asparagus
Broccoli	Turnip greens	Brussel sprouts	Collards
Cantaloupe	Winter squash	Cantaloupe	Honeydew
Carrots		Grapefruit	Kale
Chard		Green pepper	Kohlrabi
Collards		Guava	Lemon
Cress		Mango	Melon
Kale		Oranges	Potatoes
Mango		Papaya	Raw cabbage
Persimmons		Strawberries	Spinach
Pumpkin		Sweet red pepper	Sweet potatoes
Spinach			Tangerine
Sweet potatoes			Tomatoes
			Turnip greens
			Watermelon

Hints for Stretching Your Food Dollar

A large part of your monthly expenses are for food and food related items. For this reason, it is important to plan your food expenditures very carefully in order to make the most of the money you have budgeted for this expense. Some useful hints for stretching your food dollar are offered here.

1. Buy less expensive cuts of meat whenever possible. They have the same nutrition value.

2. Buy whole chickens and cut them up yourself. An investment in a good pair of kitchen boning shears will save you many dollars on the cost of cut-up chicken.

3. Make your own chicken or turkey or beef broth from the bones of these meats.

4. Use food coupons whenever possible. Make it a habit to coupon hunt each week in the newspaper. Then store them in an accordion folder by category, so they are easy to find when you go shopping.

5. Buy generic brands of foods whenever possible.

6. Rather than buy one spice or one special item for a recipe, use the substitution chart on the package to avoid unnecessary expenditures.

7. Rather than buy a new sized dish for a recipe, use one similar in size and alter your cooking time accordingly. For instance:
   — If you are substituting a pan that is shallower than the pan in the recipe, reduce the baking time by about one-quarter.
   — If you are substituting a pan that is deeper than the pan in the recipe, increase the baking time by about one-quarter.

8. PLAN YOUR MEALS BEFORE GOING TO THE GROCERY STORE. This will save you a great deal of money and will eliminate wasting a lot of food and money.

9. Never go grocery shopping when you are hungry. You tend to buy much more and especially more snack foods when you are hungry.

10. Whenever possible, do not buy prepackaged food products. These are much more expensive than making the same dish yourself. Also home prepared foods are more nutritious because they have more vitamins and no additives.

11. Buy items in bulk that store easily and offer greater cost savings. Consider shopping with a friend or group of friends at a discount warehouse and dividing up the bulk items.

12. Buy fruits and vegetables that are "in season."

Interview your parents and list their additional cost saving strategies below:

Planning Your Weekly Meals

Pretend you are 29 years old and you are planning the weekly menu for the family you described on page 77 of **Career Choices**. Remember the basic food groups and nutritional needs of your family members. Think of food as you would gasoline for your car. If you put quality gas in your car, it will perform better and last longer. If you put nutritious food in your body, you will perform better and you will live longer.

An example of a menu for Monday might be:

	Breakfast	Lunch	Dinner
Monday	Hot cereal Orange juice Toast	Tuna sandwich Apple Milk	Broiled chicken Baked potato Corn on the cob Green salad

To get started list all your favorite foods here:

Breakfast foods	Lunch	Dinner
_____	_____	_____
_____	_____	_____
_____	_____	_____
_____	_____	_____
_____	_____	_____

Snacks	Beverages	Desserts
_____	_____	_____
_____	_____	_____
_____	_____	_____
_____	_____	_____
_____	_____	_____

Hint:

If you have chosen to live on the thrifty or low-cost plan, you might consider planning meals with left-over possibilities, such as roast chicken one night, chicken salad the next night and chicken salad sandwiches for lunch the third day. That way you can buy in quantity at lower costs.

What is your idea of good nutrition and an appealing diet? Plan a week's menu.

Menu for _____ adult(s) _____ children

	Breakfast	Lunch	Dinner
Monday			
Tuesday			
Wednesday			
Thursday			
Friday			
Saturday			
Sunday			

Sample Grocery Shopping List

PRODUCE DEPARTMENT
- Fruit
- Vegetables

BAKERY
- Bread
- Rolls
- Desserts and Sweets

DAIRY PRODUCTS/DELICATESSEN
- Milk Products
- Butter or Margarine
- Yogurt
- Lunch Meats
- Cheeses
- Eggs

MEAT/FISH DEPARTMENT
- Packaged Meats (Frozen or Fresh)
- Packaged Chicken (Frozen or Fresh)
- Fish (Frozen or Fresh)

CANNED FOODS
- Fruits
- Vegetables
- Soups
- Canned Sauces

PACKAGED GOODS
- Flour, Beans, Pasta
- Cereals
- Coffee and Tea

BOTTLED/CANNED DRINKS
- Soft Drinks
- Juices
- Water

Sample Sundry Shopping List

HOUSEHOLD PRODUCT
- Cleaning Products
- Paper Goods
  (Napkins, Paper Towels, Toilet Paper)
- Laundry Detergent

SUNDRIES
- Shampoo and Hair Products
- Deodorant
- Shaving Cream
- Sunscreen
- Over-the-counter Medications and Vitamins

Write your weekly shopping list here. Include quantities. Use your menus from the **previous** page as a guide.

Find Your Weekly Grocery Costs — Part One

Make up a shopping list that reflects the ingredients needed for the menus on the preceding page. For each section, list each item you plan to buy, the quantity and the cost of each item. Then figure the total cost in column C by multiplying column A by column B.

For Example

DESCRIPTION	QUANTITY	COST PER UNIT	TOTAL COST
5 lb. bag potatoes	1	$1.39	$1.39
Low fat yogurt	3	$1.19	$3.57
1 lb. box pasta	2	$1.29	$2.58

DESCRIPTION	A QUANTITY		B COST PER UNIT		C TOTAL COST
Produce: _____	_____	X	$ _____	=	$ _____
_____	_____	X	$ _____	=	$ _____
_____	_____	X	$ _____	=	$ _____
_____	_____	X	$ _____	=	$ _____
_____	_____	X	$ _____	=	$ _____
Bakery: _____					
_____	_____	X	$ _____	=	$ _____
_____	_____	X	$ _____	=	$ _____
Dairy Products/Deli:					
_____	_____	X	$ _____	=	$ _____
_____	_____	X	$ _____	=	$ _____
_____	_____	X	$ _____	=	$ _____
_____	_____	X	$ _____	=	$ _____
Meats & Fish: _____					
_____	_____	X	$ _____	=	$ _____
_____	_____	X	$ _____	=	$ _____
_____	_____	X	$ _____	=	$ _____
Canned Goods: _____					
_____	_____	X	$ _____	=	$ _____
_____	_____	X	$ _____	=	$ _____
Bottled/Canned Drinks:					
_____	_____	X	$ _____	=	$ _____

Part One Total (Column C) $ _____

Multiply by 4 for Monthly Total   __**X** 4__

Total Monthly Cost of Part One $ _____ (D)

*See page 49 for explanation.

Monthly Costs — Part Two

code

DESCRIPTION	A QUANTITY		B COST PER UNIT		C TOTAL COST
Packaged Goods: _____	_____	X	$ _____	=	$ _____
_____	_____	X	$ _____	=	$ _____
_____	_____	X	$ _____	=	$ _____
_____	_____	X	$ _____	=	$ _____
_____	_____	X	$ _____	=	$ _____
_____	_____	X	$ _____	=	$ _____
_____	_____	X	$ _____	=	$ _____
Household Products: _____	_____	X	$ _____	=	$ _____
_____	_____	X	$ _____	=	$ _____
_____	_____	X	$ _____	=	$ _____
_____	_____	X	$ _____	=	$ _____
_____	_____	X	$ _____	=	$ _____
_____	_____	X	$ _____	=	$ _____
_____	_____	X	$ _____	=	$ _____
Sundries: _____	_____	X	$ _____	=	$ _____
_____	_____	X	$ _____	=	$ _____
_____	_____	X	$ _____	=	$ _____
_____	_____	X	$ _____	=	$ _____
_____	_____	X	$ _____	=	$ _____
_____	_____	X	$ _____	=	$ _____

Part Two Total (Column C) $ _____

Part One Monthly Total   + $ _____ (D)

Monthly Total Grocery Bill $ _____

Enter this figure for food and sundries on page 13, line 4 of Your Budget Profile.

Food Budgeting

Substitutions for a Missing Ingredient

When Recipe Calls for:	You May Substitute:
1 square unsweetened chocolate	3 tablespoons cocoa plus ½ teaspoon butter or margarine
1 cup sifted cake flour	1 cup minus 2 tablespoons sifted all purpose flour
1 tablespoon cornstarch (for thickening)	2 tablespoons flour
1 teaspoon baking powder	¼ teaspoon baking soda plus ½ teaspoon cream of tartar
1 cup sweet milk	½ cup evaporated milk plus ½ cup water
1 cup buttermilk or sour milk	1 tablespoon vinegar plus enough sweet milk to make 1 cup
¾ cup cracker crumbs	1 cup bread crumbs
1 cup brown sugar (packed)	1 cup white sugar or 1 cup sugar plus 2 tablespoons molasses
1 teaspoon lemon juice	¼ teaspoon vinegar
¼ cup chopped onion	1 tablespoon instant minced onion
1 clove garlic	⅛ teaspoon garlic powder
1 cup tomato juice	½ cup tomato sauce plus ½ cup water
1 tablespoon fresh herbs	1 teaspoon dried herbs
1 tablespoon prepared mustard	1 teaspoon dry mustard
½ cup (1 stick) butter	7 tablespoons vegetable shortening
10 miniature marshmallows	1 large marshmallow
1 medium banana	1 cup mashed bananas
1 cup beef or chicken broth	1 bouillon cube plus 1 cup boiling water
1 cup honey	1¼ cups sugar plus ¼ cup water
fresh parsley	celery tops
wine vinegar	cider vinegar

IMPORTANT MEASUREMENT EQUIVALENTS

Measure	Equivalent
Dash or Pinch	Less than ⅛ teaspoon
½ tablespoon	1½ teaspoons
1 tablespoon	3 teaspoons
1 ounce liquid	2 tablespoons
1 jigger	1½ ounces
¼ cup	4 tablespoons = 2 ounces
⅓ cup	5 tablespoons plus 1 teaspoon
½ cup	8 tablespoons = 4 ounces
⅔ cup	10 tablespoons plus 2 teaspoons
¾ cup	12 tablespoons
1 cup	16 tablespoons = 8 ounces
1 pint	2 cups
1 quart	2 pints (or 4 cups)
1 gallon	4 quarts
1 pound	16 ounces

Group Energizer — Planning a Party

You've finished a semester of hard work and it is time to celebrate. It's decided that everyone will get together for a dinner party. Someone suggests a spaghetti dinner and your committee decides to evaluate if that is within your budget. There will be 32 people attending.

The following recipes are submitted as excellent party food. Your task is to:

   a. Complete a shopping list for the party.

   b. Find out how much the food will cost for the party.

   c. Decide how much each person will need to contribute toward food costs.

"Real" Italian Spaghetti Sauce
serves 4 people

   6 tablespoons olive oil
   2 stalks celery (chopped into ¼" pieces)
   1 medium size onion (chopped)
   4 ounces uncooked bacon (each slice cut into 1" pieces)
   1 tablespoon chopped garlic
   ¼ ounce anchovy paste (optional)
   1 28-ounce can peeled italian style tomatoes — drained
   ¼ teaspoon dry basil
   2 tablespoons chopped canned black olives — drained

Pasta
   14 ounces of capelini or thin spaghetti pasta noodles

Utensils needed: One large frying pan, one large pot for pasta, strainer for draining pasta, large bowl for serving.

Heat olive oil on medium heat and saute onions, celery, bacon, and garlic until lightly brown. Add anchovy paste (optional), stir and add tomatoes. Chop up tomatoes as you stir and then let mixture simmer for 20 minutes. Add basil and olives 5 minutes before serving.

Cook pasta noodles from directions on package, drain, mix with sauce and serve immediately from large bowl.

Garlic Bread
serves 10 people

   ¾ cup mayonnaise
   ¾ cup grated parmesan cheese
   2 tablespoons chopped garlic
   1 loaf sourdough bread, sliced

Utensils needed: Cookie sheet, mixing bowl

Mix first three ingredients together and spread on bread. Arrange bread slices on cookie sheets and place under broiler for 30 to 60 seconds until golden brown. Watch closely so they do not burn.

Caesar Salad
serves 6 People

   1 large head red leafy lettuce — washed and chopped in one-inch strips
   1 ripe avocado — sliced
   ¼ cup grated Parmesan cheese
   2 tablespoons bacon bits — crumbled
   3 tablespoons Girard's Caesar salad dressing (or other brand caesar salad dressing)
   2 tablespoons Bernstein's Cheese Fantastico Salad Dressing (or other Italian salad dressing with cheese)

Utensils needed: Salad bowl, knife

Mix together first four ingredients. Pour on salad dressings and **toss well** just before serving.

Sun Iced Tea
serves 8 people

Utensils needed: Sun tea jar or clear glass container.

Place 4 tea bags in a large clear glass container filled with ½ gallon of water. Place in the sun for the afternoon. Serve over ice. This makes 8 eight-ounce servings.

You may choose to follow directions on the package for regular iced tea.

Note: Try these recipes...you'll love them.

FOR EXTRA, EXTRA CREDIT: Submit your own party recipes, shopping list, budget, and cost per person. Complete a chart similar to the one on pages 62 and 63, using a computerized spreadsheet.

Worksheet for Factoring Supplies Needed and Costs for your Party

Directions for Completing your Party Planner

1. After you have decided on your shopping list and the quantities needed for the recipes, you have to decide how many times to 'double' each recipe so everyone gets a portion. For example, if there are 32 people attending your party and your recipe serves 4, you will need to make 8 times that recipe. (Hint: $32 \div 4 = 8$). Place the correct number in column C for each different recipe. (Use the chart on the following page.)

2. Factor the total amount of each ingredient needed by multiplying the recipe amount with the number of times the recipe must be increased. (B × C = D)

3. Next you would need to evaluate the unit size of the item you are going to buy. For instance, if each bunch of celery has 8 stalks (average) you would write 8 stalks in column E. (*For this exercise we have completed this research for you.*)

4. In column F you will compute and write the number of units needed to be purchased. For instance, in the case of celery, you will need 2 bunches of celery.* (D ÷ E + F) Remember to round up to the next unit if you come up with a fraction or decimal. You'll have leftovers.

5. In column G you would write the price of one unit of the item. For instance, a bunch of celery costs $.89. (*For this exercise we have completed this research for you.*)

6. In column H you will factor the total cost of the celery you require. (2 bunches x $.89 = $1.78) (F x G = H)

7. When you have completed the computations of each ingredient, total column H to show your total food costs.

8. To find out how much each person owes the party committee, divide total cost of food by the number of people in attendance.

Note: If you have access to a computer in your computer lab at school, ask the instructor to show you how to set up a computer spreadsheet of this planning chart. Then with the flick of a few buttons you can change the number in attendance from 32 people to 100 people to 50 people with this skill. You're on your way to helping with a wedding reception or opening your own catering business.

*If the units of measure of the item sold at the store are not the same as those which the recipe calls for (i.e. olive oil), then you will need to convert the unit of measure found in the store. Use the Important Measurement Equivalent Chart on page 59. Place the conversion in column B on the right side.

Your Party Planner

A	B		C
Ingredient	**Recipe amount**		**Number of times recipe is needed to feed group**
Given	Given	convert * items to units of measure in column E	# of people at party ――――― # of servings/recipe
SPAGHETTI SAUCE (serves 4)			
olive oil*	6 tablespoons	= ounces	8
celery	2 stalks		8
onion	1		8
bacon	4 ounces		8
chopped garlic	1 tablespoon	ounces	8
anchovy paste (optional)	¼ ounce		8
can peeled Italian style tomatoes	28 ounces		8
basil	¼ teaspoon dry	ounces	8
sliced canned black olives	2 tablespoons	ounces	8
PASTA (serves 4)			
spaghetti pasta	14 ounces		
GARLIC BREAD (serves 10)			
mayonnaise*	¾ cup	= pint	
grated parmesan cheese	¾ cup	= ounces	
chopped garlic*	2 tablespoons	= ounces	
sourdough bread	One loaf — sliced		
CEASER SALAD (serves 6)			
red leafy lettuce	One large head		
avocado	One		
grated Parmesan cheese	¼ cup	ounces	
bacon*	2 tablespoons	= ounces	
Caesar salad dressing*	3 tablespoons	= ounces	
Italian salad dressing*	2 tablespoons	= ounces	
SUN ICE TEA (Serves 8 people)	4 bags		

*Use the Measurement Equivalent chart on page 59 to help you convert to like measurements.

⊖ ⊗ ⊕ ⊘ ⊕ ⊗ ⊗ ⊘

D total amount of ingredients needed	E standard unit size	F number of units needed	G price per unit	H total
B X C = D	Researched	D ÷ E = F	Researched	F X G = H
	12 ounces		$2.99	
	8 stalks = 1 bunch		$ .89/bunch	
	8 onions = 1 bag		$1.49/bag	
	1 pound		$1.99	
	4 ounces		$1.49	
	1¾ ounces		$1.61	
	28 ounces		$1.39	
	dry ½ ounce		$3.29	
	2¼ ounces		$ .69	
	14 ounces		$1.29	
	1 pint		$1.43	
	8 ounces		$2.86	
	4 ounces		$1.49	
	(10 slices) =1 loaf		$1.99/loaf	
	1		$ .69	
	1		$ .75	
	8 ounces		$2.85	
	2 ounces		$1.59	
	12 ounces		$3.19	
	16 ounces		$2.19	
	20 bags		$1.95	

Total Cost For Food _____

Cost Per Person _____

Monthly Entertainment Budget

What kind of entertainment do you hope to be able to pursue when you are 29 years old? What about the other members of your proposed family? We have listed a variety of activities and items here. Do not assume you need to do everything. That would stretch anyone's budget! Choose only the activities that are most appealing to you. Your newspaper's weekend entertainment section may be helpful.

DESCRIPTION OF ACTIVITY	A Number of Times or Purchases Per Month		B Average Cost Per Activity or Purchase		C Total Monthly Cost
1. Restaurants/ Dining Out	_____	X	_____	=	_____
2. Entertaining at Home	_____	X	_____	=	_____
3. Movies	_____	X	_____	=	_____
4. Concerts	_____	X	_____	=	_____
5. Video Rentals, Etc.	_____	X	_____	=	_____
6. Sporting Events	_____	X	_____	=	_____
7. Exercise or Health Club Costs	_____	X	_____	=	_____
8. Newspaper/ Magazine Subscriptions	_____	X	_____	=	_____
9. Books, Tapes, CD's, Etc.	_____	X	_____	=	_____
10. Hobbies (*list*)	_____	X	_____	=	_____
_____					
_____					
11. Children's a. Entertainment b. Memberships c. Recreation d. Lessons	_____	X	_____	=	_____
12. Participation in Sports	_____	X	_____	=	_____
13. Savings for Special Equipment such as Walkman, VCR, Stereo, CD Player	_____	X	_____	=	_____
14. Other (*describe*)	_____	X	_____	=	_____
_____					
_____					

TOTAL MONTHLY COST _____

Enter this figure on page 13, line 5 of Your Budget Profile.

Once you have figured your **total** monthly expenses for the lifestyle you would like when you are 29 (total on page 13), it is always interesting to find out how much entertainment costs are of each dollar you spend. In other words, figure what percentage your entertainment budget is of your total budget.

Entertainment Budget ÷ Total Budget x 100 = % of Total Budget that you plan to spend on entertainment.

Recreation is More Than Just Fun

Participating in recreational activities is important for your health and psychological well being. The relaxation and good feelings you experience while doing something you truly enjoy will help you maintain your enthusiasm for all the other tasks in your life. Employers find the best workers are individuals who, during their time off work, do something they enjoy. (Review page 112 of **Career Choices**.)

Many hobbies, sports and recreational pursuits have start-up costs that need careful financial planning. For example, each sport has special equipment and clothing. Some, such as horseback riding, boating and skiing require substantial outlays of money to get started. If your hobby is music, to surround yourself in the sounds of your choice will necessitate a careful savings and acquisition plan.

Choose a favorite recreational activity that you might like to explore and develop a start-up budget below. List each item needed and research its costs. If there is someone else in the class who also wants to pursue this hobby, form a team and compare notes.

Describe your ideal recreational pursuit below:

Budget

Item	Cost
_____	_____
_____	_____
_____	_____
_____	_____
_____	_____
_____	_____
_____	_____
_____	_____
_____	_____
_____	_____
_____	_____
_____	_____
_____	_____
_____	_____

TOTAL Start-up Costs _____

Depending on the financial commitments of the hobby you choose, you may have to start small, borrow or rent the items you need or purchase second-hand equipment. When you are young, many other things may be more critical to the security and well-being of your family. Write a long-range plan below. Turn back to this page when developing your savings plan on page 80.

Energizer — Math Baseball

Speaking of entertainment, the following is a game everyone will enjoy. First read the directions carefully and then form teams and begin to play.

Choosing Teams

1. Choose someone in your class who has a similar skill level in math. Pair up with this person.

2. All pairs count off with each pair receiving a number. This will be your batting order. You will always "bat" against the other person in your pair.

3. Finally the pairs will divide into two teams with a member of each pair on each team. The person you have chosen to pair with will be on the other team. One team will sit or line up on one side of the room and the other team on the other side of the room.

What Do You Need to Play?

4. Place four bases around the room in a diamond shape like a baseball field with home plate at the front of the room.

5. You'll need three stacks of math problem flash cards, each varying in difficulty. Your instructor will provide these.

> BUSH LEAGUE —This group of flash cards is designed to challenge the students in the class who have basic math skills.

> FARM LEAGUE — This group of flash cards is for students with the next level of difficulty.

> MAJOR LEAGUE — This group of flash cards will challenge the students in the class who have the most advanced math skills.

6. You need to keep score of the innings, outs, and runs. The chalkboard or over-head projector can be used for keeping track of the score.

7. Finally you need a person to be the pitcher. This could be the teacher or, if you have an odd number of students in the class, it could be the extra student. The pitcher is stationed at the front of the room facing the class, so when he/she pulls the flash card the whole class is able to see it.

How To Play

8. The game is played with the same rules as baseball. There are 9 innings, one team is "at bat" and one team is "in the field" (either sitting in their seats or standing at opposite sides of the room). After three outs, the batting side retires (to their seats or side). Points are scored when a runner crosses "homeplate."

9. Each pair (from opposite teams, in batting order) goes to the front of the room and faces the pitcher. (Their backs will be to the class.) The person representing the at bat team stands slightly forward, while the person in the field plays in the same position as the catcher would. The pair decides from which pile (Bush League, Farm League, Major League) the pitcher will pull a flash card. If the pair can't agree, then each player makes the choice every other time as they rotate at bat.

10. The flash card is drawn and the player who first answers it correctly determines the play. If the player batting answers correctly first, that player advances to first base. If the catcher answers correctly first, the batter is out.

    a. If the first person to answer calls out a wrong answer, then the play goes to the other team. For example, if the batter answers incorrectly, that player is out. If the catcher's answer is wrong, the batter goes to first base.

    b. If neither player answers, (both do not know the answer or are unwilling to guess), the pitcher calls out a number that represents one of the other pair's batting order number. The first person from **that** pair who is the correct respondent to the same question determines the play. Therefore everyone must pay attention to each play in case their number is called.

    c. A foul play occurs when one of the other team members calls out the answer out of turn. If that happens, the opposing team is awarded that play.

11. Players at bat continue to advance, one base at a time as each successful batter moves to first base until the side is retired with 3 outs. Runs are scored each time a player crosses home plate.

12. The team with the most runs at the end of the game wins. Before the game starts decide the number of innings which constitute a completed game.

Saving and Planning for a Vacation

Read page 87 of **Career Choices** for a description of vacation alternatives. Choose the best description of the type and timing of vacations that you imagine would appeal to you when you are 29 years old.

Complete the following worksheet to determine your monthly savings for your vacation.
(Hint — get copies of Sunday's newspaper travel section for ads showing typical costs.)

Monthly Vacation Budget Worksheet

Describe the type of vacation you plan to take:

_____

_____

_____

How many days will you spend on this vacation? _____

How often do you hope to take vacations? _____

Will family members accompany you? _____ Who? _____

Expenses of the Proposed Vacation

Estimate all your expenses.

1. Airfare, Train Fare, or Other Public Transportation (describe) _____

   _____

Number of people	X	Cost of ticket	=	Total public transportation cost
_____	X	$ _____	=	$ _____

2. Car Rental

Cost/day or week	X	Number of days or weeks	=	Car rental cost
$ _____	X	_____	=	$ _____

3. Personal Car Expense *(figure mileage costs based on $.40 per mile)*

Number of miles	X	$.40/mile	=	Automobile costs
_____	X	_____	=	$ _____

4. Hotel, Motel, Condo, Cabin, Campground or Other Lodging Costs

(describe) _____

Number of days	X	Cost/night	=	Lodging costs
_____	X	$ _____	=	$ _____

5. Food
Will you: eat out, cook, or buy a vacation package with food included?

Number of people	X	Number of days	X	Average cost/day	=	Food costs
_____	X	_____	X	$ _____	=	$ _____

6. Entertainment/Activities (Describe) _____
(such as zoo, boat rental, Disneyland, etc.)

Number of people	X Average cost per activity =	Activity costs
_____	X $ _____ =	$ _____

Number of people	X Average cost per activity =	Activity costs
_____	X $ _____ =	$ _____

7. Souvenirs (Describe) _____

What will be your budget for souvenirs? $ _____

8. Other _____ $ _____

                                    Total Cost $ _____ A

Saving for Your Vacation

How much must you save per month to meet your vacation goal $ _____ B
if you plan to take an annual vacation?

> Divide total cost by 12 if you plan to take an annual vacation.
> A ÷ 12 = B

                    Enter B on page 13, line 6 of Your Budget Profile.

If you planned to take this type of vacation every two years, how would you determine the amount of monthly savings you would require?

If you planned to take this type of vacation twice a year, how would you determine the amount of monthly savings you would need?

Creative Planning

Join together with 3 to 5 classmates to find a creative solution to this dilemma.

Your vacation time has arrived, but when you check your bank statement you find you can only afford to spend $120 on your holiday. You've had a number of unexpected expenses this year that required you to dip into your vacation savings. But you are creative . . . you are not going to let this block your need for rest, relaxation and fun. Design a seven-day vacation that gives you the chance to have some fun.

Describe your vacation here:

Outline your budget:

	Describe	Cost
Transportation	_____	$_____
Lodging	_____	$_____
Food	_____	$_____
Activity costs	_____	$_____
Souvenirs	_____	$_____
Other	_____	$_____
Total		$ 120.00

Describe how you were resourceful and realized savings:

Child Care Budget

1. Read page 88 in *Career Choices* for a summary of child care options and related expenses. Choose the option you think you will use for child care.

2. Complete the following worksheet for a child care budget for the following three possibilities:

   A. 1 child – age 1

   B. 1 child – age 1
      1 child – age 3

   C. 2 children – age 2
      1 child – age 7

Assume in all cases the children under school age will need child care from 7:30 AM to 5:30 PM five days per week for a total of 50 hours per week. Assume the 7-year-old will need care from 2:30 PM to 5:30 PM five days per week for a total of 15 hours per week. Assume the living expenses for live-in help (housing, food, transportation) is $100/week.

WORKSHEET FOR WEEKLY CHILD CARE BUDGET

	A	B	C
Children	1 Child, Age 1	1 Child, Age 1 1 Child, Age 3	2 Children, Age 2 1 Child, Age 7
Housekeeper (live-in) Living expenses/week	Hrs.　Rate　Subtotal 50 X $3.67 = $_____ 　　　+ $100 Total Cost $_____	Hrs.　Rate　Subtotal 50 X $3.67 = $_____ 　　　+ $100 Total Cost $_____	Hrs.　Rate　Subtotal 50 X $3.67 = $_____ 　　　+ $100 Total Cost $_____
Day Care Center	Hrs.　Rate　Subtotal 50 X $2.45 = $_____ Total Cost $_____	Hrs.　Rate　Subtotal 50 X $2.45 = $_____ 50 X $1.94 = $_____ Total Cost $_____	Hrs.　Rate　Subtotal 50 X $2.45 = $_____ 50 X $2.45 = $_____ 15 X $1.94 = $_____ Total Cost $_____

For purposes of this exercise, assume the hourly child care cost for a school age child is the same as for a preschooler (age 3).

Describe other options for child care.

3. After you have completed the worksheet, answer these questions regarding how the following scenarios could change your monthly child care costs:

A. Your 3-year-old child has chicken pox and can't go to the day care center for one week. You must stay home from work without pay to care for your child. What impact does this have on your income?

Fact: You earn $13.83/hour and work full-time (40 hours/week).

B. Your private day care provider takes a vacation for three weeks each July. How do you plan to cover child care during this time? List your options? Circle the option you think would be best for you and your child(ren).

C. What other situations or factors might affect your child care arrangements? What would be the financial impact of these? Explain here.

4. Dependent Care — Read page 88 of *Career Choices* and complete this section if this situation could apply to you.

5. Now complete a child care budget for your projected family when you are 29 years old, taking into account the number of children and their ages as well as the type of desired child care.

Projected number of children at age 29 (from page 12) _____

Child	Their age	Describe each child's child care needs
_____	_____	_____
_____	_____	_____
_____	_____	_____
_____	_____	_____

Show your calculations here for figuring your weekly child care costs

Child	Hours/Week		Rate/Hour		Subtotal
_____	_____	X	$_____	=	$_____
_____	_____	X	$_____	=	$_____
_____	_____	X	$_____	=	$_____
_____	_____	X	$_____	=	$_____
				Weekly Total	$_____

Now figure monthly cost by multiplying your weekly total by 4 and enter your total child care costs on page 13, line 7 of Your Budget Profile.

Health Care Budget

Read "Health Care" on page 89 in *Career Choices*. To help plan your annual health care budget, it is necessary to consider different expenses you could face. Complete the following worksheet, taking into account projected annual expenses for your future family.

Part One — Yearly Out-of-Pocket Expenses

Cold tablets and cough syrups $_____

Eye glasses/contact lenses $_____

Bandages/band-aids $_____

Creams and ointments $_____

Headache medications $_____

Digestion medications $_____

Health insurance payments (through work) $_____

Other _____ $_____

A. Total yearly out-of-pocket expenses $_____(A)

Part Two — Items That May Be Covered by Medical Insurance

Emergency care $_____

Hospital care $_____

Doctor's office visits $_____

Prescriptions $_____

Visits to dentist $_____

Orthodontics $_____

Visits to family counselors $_____

Other _____ $_____

B. Total annual costs of which a portion is covered by insurance $_____(B)

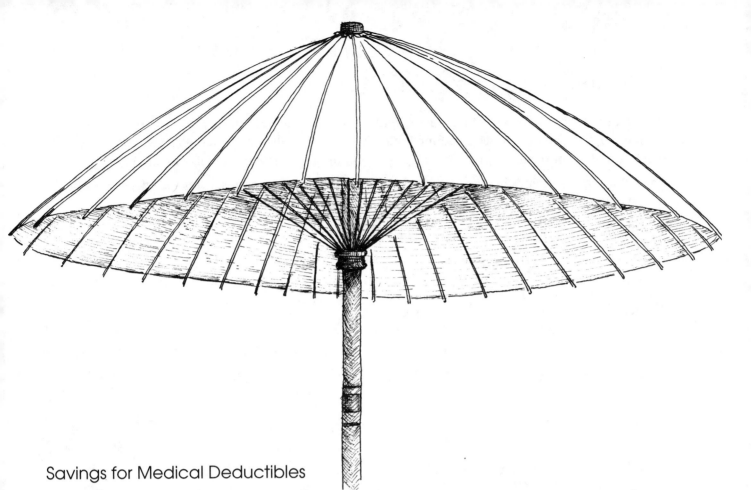

Savings for Medical Deductibles

The items on the previous page are listed in two parts. For the items in Part One, you must set aside a monthly amount to cover the cost of these items. In Part Two, employers' medical insurance will cover some of these costs, usually a percentage. Since medical plans vary, some are more complete in their coverage of these expenses. Most plans require a portion of expenses be paid by the individual. Therefore it is necessary to set aside a monthly amount to cover these costs.

A good rule of thumb is to set aside twenty percent (20%) of the total costs estimated in Part Two. For this exercise, let's assume you have good medical insurance coverage at your place of work. Therefore you may only be responsible for 20% of covered costs in Part Two.

C. 20% of total of Part Two $_____
      B × .20 = C

Add total out-of-pocket expenses (A) $_____

D. Total annual health care costs $_____
      A + C = D

E. Divide by 12 to find monthly budget for health care costs $_____
      D ÷ 12 = E

Enter monthly budget figures for health care on page 13, line 8 of Your Budget Profile.

Furnishings Expenses

Read "Furnishings" on page 89 in **Career Choices**. For this exercise assume you have the majority of the major items you need to set up a functioning household by the time you are 29 years old. Below you will budget for replacement items and major new appliances you would like to purchase.

The following is Morgan's budget for repairs and replacements. Morgan is a very handy person who, with the help of a fix-it manual, can perform most simple repairs.

MORGAN'S BUDGET

REPLACEMENT ITEMS

Linens (Sheets, Towels, etc.)	$20 per year
Kitchen Items	$30 per year
Miscellaneous	$20 per year
Total	$70 per year

SAVINGS FOR REPAIRS

Repair of: Washer/Dryer	$20 per year
Refrigerator/Stove	$10 per year
Hot Water Heater	$15 per year
TV/Stereo	$10 per year
Vacuum Cleaner	$ 5 per year
Miscellaneous	$ 5 per year
Total	$65 per year

SAVINGS FOR MAJOR PURCHASES

Morgan plans to save $1000 this year for the purchase of a new major appliance or furnishing.

Your Annual Budget For Repairs/Replacements/Major Purchases

What household furnishings would you like to purchase? List each item and estimated cost. The total is the amount that needs to be put in reserve for the coming year.

Description of Item or Reserve: Cost

_____ $_____

_____ $_____

_____ $_____

_____ $_____

_____ $_____

_____ $_____

_____ $_____

_____ $_____

_____ $_____

_____ $_____

_____ $_____

_____ $_____

                  Annual Total $_____

Now divide the total by 12 to calculate the amount per month and enter your monthly total on page 13, line 9 of Your Budget Profile.

                  Monthly Total $_____

Form a group with 3 to 5 classmates to brainstorm the following problem.

Figuring Depreciation

You might be wondering how much you need to save each year for major purchases. Rather than guess on an average figure as Morgan did, you can be much more accurate in your planning. As businesses do, you can set up a depreciation schedule and save according to a plan.

What Is Depreciation?

Depreciation is the amount an item loses in value as it ages or is used up. For instance, cars depreciate each year based on model year, mileage, and condition. We know a 1998 car is worth more than the same model 1997 car. The same thing is true for almost all major durable goods.

Eventually an item depreciates to the point it no longer has value. It is either used up, worn out or out of style or date. Therefore, each category of item has a "life span" which is the average number of years that type of an item is serviceable. For instance, a refrigerator's average life span might be 15 years while a vacuum cleaner's life span might be 8 years.

Figuring Your Own Depreciation Schedule (and Savings Needs)

To figure how much you will need to save each year to replace the household items **you already have in your home**, complete the chart on the next page.

In column A list all the household appliances and pieces of furniture you think you will own when you are 29 years old.

In column B estimate the cost of each item. (Display advertisements from newspapers and catalogs will help.)

In column C guess or research the lifespan of each item. How often do you think each will need to be replaced?

Divide the cost of the item by the lifespan to come up with the annual depreciation figure. Enter that figure for each item in column D.

Total column D to learn your annual depreciation.

This is the amount you must save annually so you can replace household items as they wear out.

Savings Plan for Replacement Purchases

A Item	B Cost	C ÷ Lifespan	D Annual Depreciation (B/C = D)	
	$	yrs.	$	/yr.
	$	yrs.	$	/yr.
	$	yrs.	$	/yr.
	$	yrs.	$	/yr.
	$	yrs.	$	/yr.
	$	yrs.	$	/yr.
	$	yrs.	$	/yr.
	$	yrs.	$	/yr.
	$	yrs.	$	/yr.
	$	yrs.	$	/yr.
	$	yrs.	$	/yr.
	$	yrs.	$	/yr.
	$	yrs.	$	/yr.
	$	yrs.	$	/yr.
	$	yrs.	$	/yr.
Total Annual Depreciation			$	/yr.

Saving for the Long Term

Read the section on saving on page 89 in *Career Choices*. Then read and study the following example.

Example of Morgan's Saving Plan

Description	Annual Savings Amount	Monthly Amount
Emergencies	$120.00	$ 10.00
Major Repairs, Replacement	$ 60.00	$ 5.00
Major Purchases	$120.00	$ 10.00
Children's College Education	$300.00	$ 25.00
Retirement, IRA's	$300.00	$ 25.00
Income Reserve	$300.00	$ 25.00
Other (Undefined)	$120.00	$ 10.00
Total	$1320.00	$110.00

Now complete *your* annual saving plan. Calculate your monthly savings amount by dividing each item by 12.

Savings Plan

Description	Annual Savings Amount		Monthly savings
Emergencies	$_____	÷ 12 =	$_____
Major repairs, replacement	$_____	÷ 12 =	$_____
Major purchases (new equipment/ furnishings)	$_____	÷ 12 =	$_____
Child(ren)'s college education	$_____	÷ 12 =	$_____
Retirement, IRA's	$_____	÷ 12 =	$_____
Income Cushion	$_____	÷ 12 =	$_____
Other	$_____	÷ 12 =	$_____
Total Savings	$_____	÷ 12 =	$_____

Enter the total monthly savings to be budgeted on page 13, line 10 of Your Budget Profile.

What Percentage of Your Salary Must You Save Per Month?

Financial planners recommend that individuals save at least 5% of their net pay per month. Review the findings from your survey on pages 34 and 35 of *Career Choices*. If security was one of your top values you may want to consider a figure more like 10% to 15%.

It is important that you have a target figure (usually a percentage) and a plan.

You will turn back and complete this page after you complete page 85.

Your Plan

Once you have figured your required monthly net pay (the amount required to cover your monthly expenses, which is line item 12 on page 13), come back and figure the percentage of savings required each month to meet your needs.

Formula:

To find your percentage of savings, divide your monthly savings amount required (from page 80) by your monthly net pay (from page 13).

Monthly savings required ÷ Monthly net pay = Percentage of savings

Percentage of savings you required _____%

Is this percentage realistic? If it is more than 15%, what other options do you have? Write your plan below.

Interview parents, relatives, friends and mentors. Ask them what percentage of their wages they save. They can give you this figure (the percentage) without disclosing personal financial information. How did they make their decision on the percentage amount? What is their savings plan and philosophy?

Group Think

Form a group of 3 to 5 classmates to discuss and solve these problems.

Estimate how much you need to save to meet the long-term savings goals described below. Given the following information, calculate how much you will need to budget each year and each month to meet the savings goal.

Retirement Savings

You are 25 years old. You want to retire when you are 62 years old. Between now and then you want to put a total of $100,000 into a retirement savings account. Remember your account will have more money in it due to interest earned (see page 209 of **Career Choices** for an example of what that can mean). How much will you need to save each year, and how much will you need to save each month?

Each year $ _____

Each month $ _____

How much will you need to earn per month if you plan to save 10% of your salary for retirement to meet your $100,000 goal? What annual salary would be required?

Earnings each month $ _____

Earnings each year $ _____

Saving for College

Your 5-year-old child is very bright and eager to learn. You would like to be able to send your child to college when he/she is 18 years old. After some research, you decide that you will need to save $16,000 from your paychecks between now and then to provide enough support. (You expect the $16,000 to earn an average annual interest rate of 7%, and you also expect your child to attend a state university and contribute part of expenses through summer earnings, loans, and scholarships.) How much do you need to save for college, each month and each year, to reach your goal?

Each year $ _____

Each month $ _____

Income Reserve

You are currently earning $18,000 per year. You want to build up an income cushion over the next four years that equals four months' salary in case you lose your job, become ill for an extended period or have to care for an older family member. How much will you need to save each month to meet this savings goal?

Amount of savings required each month to meet income cushion goal $ _____

This equals what percentage of your monthly salary? $ _____

Making Choices

You could probably buy a new economy car with monthly payments about the same amount as your monthly savings for your four-month income cushion (indicated above).

You currently have a used car that runs well if given the proper care. Which would be more important to you: a new car or the peace of mind of knowing you have a savings cushion in case you lose your job and can't find work for a long period? Ask each person in the group to share his/her thoughts and choices.

Miscellaneous Expenses

Read page 90 in *Career Choices*.

Consider what expenses you might have on a regular or occasional basis that you have not included in a previous worksheet. Some of those areas of miscellaneous expense might be:

MISCELLANEOUS EXPENSES	ANNUAL COSTS		MONTHLY COSTS
All costs related to pets	$_____	÷ 12 =	$_____

    Purchase of pet food
    Veterinary bills
    Pet toys
    Beds, cages, aquariums, etc.

Holiday gifts, shower and wedding presents, birthday gifts	$_____	÷ 12 =	$_____
Contributions to community, social, or religious affiliations	$_____	÷ 12 =	$_____
Private schools for your children	$_____	÷ 12 =	$_____
Internet connections	$_____	÷ 12 =	$_____
Other miscellaneous expenses			
_____	$_____	÷ 12 =	$_____
_____	$_____	÷ 12 =	$_____
_____	$_____	÷ 12 =	$_____
	$_____	÷ 12 =	$_____
	Total Annual Costs		Total Monthly Costs

Enter your total monthly estimate for miscellaneous expenses on page 13, line 11 of Your Budget Profile.

÷ +

Your Total Budget Profile

1. Read page 92 in *Career Choices*. Now that you have completed all the exercises related to preparing your personal budget, it it time to complete page 13 of this book to determine your projected total budget.

2. Review all the budget exercises again. If you haven't already, enter the monthly amounts you calculated for the expense categories on page 13:

	From page(s)
Housing [1]	17
Transportation [2]	33, 36, 40, 41
Clothing [3]	44, 45, 46, 47
Food and Sundries [4]	57
Entertainment [5]	64
Vacations [6]	69
Child Care [7]	73
Health Care [8]	75
Furnishings [9]	77
Savings [10]	80
Miscellaneous [11]	84

3. Add these eleven (11) amounts to determine your total monthly budget.

The total monthly expense of the lifestyle I envision for myself at age 29 is $ _____

From page 13, line 12

This is a very important number. It is the minimum amount of money you need to have each month after taxes and deductions are taken from your paycheck to live the lifestyle you envision. In other words, this is your required take-home salary or net pay.

What Ends Up In Your Pocket

Read page 93 in *Career Choices* again. The monthly budget amount you have just calculated is the amount of money you will need to **bring home in your paycheck** after taxes, social security, worker's compensation, and any other deductions such as medical insurance. You will need to calculate the gross pay required to meet your budget.

For the purpose of this exercise, assume that the amount withheld for taxes
and other deductions will be 20%.

Review the following examples before calculating your own gross pay requirements.

Let's say you completed your budget profile and found you needed $2,500 per month to meet your lifestyle expectations when you are 29 years old. That means you have to "take home" $2,500 per month. But how do you find out what salary you need to earn?

With a monthly budget of $2,500, the calculation to determine required gross pay is as follows:

> If 20% of your pay is deducted from your salary, then you have 80% left to take home.
> Therefore, for this problem, 80% of total salary = take home salary
> Let's use ratios to figure this out.

$$\frac{\$2,500}{80\%} = \frac{X}{100\%}$$

The above formula is read: $2,500 is to 80% as X (the unknown) is to 100%

Your task is to find out what X is. X stands for the total salary (100%) required. You can compute this when you already know the percentage amount of the total ($2,500 is 80% of the total salary).

Ask your instructor to explain ratios and how to compute. You'll use them often.

Now you can complete the equation to find out what X is.

$$\frac{\text{Take home salary}}{80\%} = \text{Total salary required}$$

$2,500 divided by 80%   or $2,500/.80   or $2,500 ÷ .80 = $3,125.00

$3,125 is the monthly salary you must earn to take home $2,500 per month in your paycheck

  Career Choices .com

Your Annual Salary Requirement

Using your figure from your monthly budget (page 13, line 12) calculate your own monthly salary requirement assuming there are 20% deductions from your paycheck. (See page 85 for an explanation.)

$$\underset{\text{Take home salary}}{\underline{\hspace{4cm}}} \div\ .80\ =\ \underset{\text{Monthly salary required}}{\underline{\hspace{4cm}}}$$

What **annual** salary is required to meet your budget? (Multiply your monthly salary requirement by 12). Remember, this is **your** budget and the annual salary figure required to support *your* personal lifestyle.

$ _____ your annual salary
requirement

You will want to memorize this figure. It will be one of the important pieces of information to consider as you make decisions about the career you want and the resources of time, energy and money you want to commit to prepare for that career.

> The preceding calculations are important mathematical computations that are worth learning. If you want to be able to make the best decisions for yourself and your family, keep trying until you understand this process. This is powerful information and essential knowledge.

If you still don't understand this, ask your instructor to provide you with practice problems until you do. Remember, math is not a talent you are born with. It is a skill to be learned.

Find a Job That Will Support Your Lifestyle

Enter your annual salary requirement from page 87 here $ _____

> Now find a job **you think you will be qualified for** that will support the lifestyle you envision.

You'll want to research the wages of interesting careers. There are various books, computer programs, and web sites available, so ask your career technician or librarian for assistance.

Our favorite resource is the *Occupational Outlook Handbook*. Produced by the U.S. Department of Labor and updated every two years, a print edition is published by Jist Works. You can also access the information online through the Bureau of Labor Statistics' web site at http://www.bls.gov/oco/. Either way, it is a treasure trove of information.

From your research, list 10 occupations that will support your lifestyle.

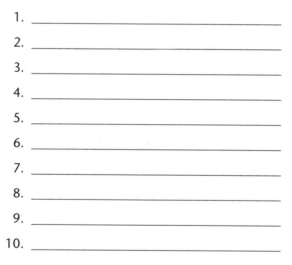

1. _____
2. _____
3. _____
4. _____
5. _____
6. _____
7. _____
8. _____
9. _____
10. _____

Star any of the occupations that you think might be of interest to you **and** for which you are willing to complete the necessary education.

If you have trouble finding appropriate careers that would support your desired lifestyle, what other options do you have?

Computing Salaries In Your Head — Quickly!

Imagine you have just accepted a job and are finalizing your employment agreement with your new boss. During your first interview, several days earlier, you stated the minimum wage you would accept was $9.00 per hour. At that time your new employer agreed to this. As you look at your contract you note you are being offered an annual salary of $17,000 per year. What is your response?

If you were the above boss, what would be a convincing argument for you?

The company you work for is restructuring. Your department has been eliminated and you are being moved to the position of administrative director for a similar division. Your boss calls you in to read the job description. When you review it you discover it is essentially the same work as your previous position, only now you will be classified as a manager and placed on an annual salary rather than hourly wage. As you finish reading your boss abruptly asks, "What are your yearly salary expectations?" If your previous wages were $12.45 per hour, what should be your minimum expectations?

$_____

What kind of response would you likely get if you asked for $30,000?

While interviewing a prospective employee for a job in your company, you eventually get the the standard questions of compensation (pay). The conversation goes like this:

> You: *What did you make at your last job?*
>
> Interviewee: *$11.00 per hour*
>
> You: *What are your financial requirements?*
>
> Interviewee: *I want to make what I made at my previous job.*
>
> You: *This position pays between $22,000 and $26,000 per year depending on experience. How does that sound to you?*
>
> Interviewee: *I must make $26,000 per year, like I made before.*

What is wrong here? Would this person continue to be a candidate for the position? Why or why not?

Numbers To Memorize

As you begin planning for a career, you will want to become very comfortable working with certain numbers. These special numbers should be memorized because they will come up over and over again, sometimes when you least expect it.

If you become comfortable with these numbers and calculations, you will feel more secure as you negotiate with a new employer or bargin for a raise. You will be able to calculate quickly in your head and therefore can respond with confidence and conviction.

Factoring Hourly Wage Into Annual Wage

One of the most important numbers you need to memorize is how many hours there are in a work year.

Formula

52 weeks/year X 40 hours/week = 2,080 work hours/year

For factoring hourly wage into annual compensation **QUICKLY,** we suggest you round this number to **2,000 hours/year.**

The math skills involved are:

Estimation

Averaging

Rounding to the nearest whole

Below we have collected the median hourly wages for a variety of positions and rounded them to the nearest dollar. See how quickly you can calculate the annual salary for the following jobs using the 2,000 hour average rule. (Ask a classmate to time you.)

Job	Median hourly wage	Estimated annual salary
Fast Food Counter Worker	$7.00 per hour	_____
Telephone Operator	$14.00 per hour	_____
Janitor	$10.00	_____
Construction Equipment Operator	$17.00	_____
Aircraft Mechanic	$22.00	_____
Writer or Author	$22.00	_____

Now round the hourly rates below to the nearest whole dollar and then compute as estimated annual salary (using the 2,000 rule). Again, the task is to do this quickly, so time yourself.

Job	Median hourly wage	Estimated annual salary
Registered Nurse	$25.79	_____
Federal Tax Examiner	$27.90	_____
Hospital Chaplain	$24.84	_____
Air Traffic Controller	$49.22	_____
Mathematician	$38.95	_____
General Engineer	$36.59	_____
Physicist	$42.06	_____
Lawyer, General	$46.83	_____
Hospital Administrator	$37.73	_____
Dentist	$58.86	_____

Practice this activity a number of times over the next few weeks, timing yourself with each try. In the future, when someone quotes you an hourly wage, you can immediately transpose it to annual compensation. And, because you know your annual budget requirements, you'll be able to evaluate the feasibility of that job for you.

SOURCE: *U.S. Bureau of Labor Statistics, Division of Occupational Employment Statistics, National Occupational Employment and Wage Estimates,* November 2004.

Group Think

Form a study group of 3 to 5 of your classmates.

Study the table of average **annual** expenditures for various sized families on page 94 of *Career Choices*. How does each of your budgets compare to this chart?

Remember that in order to compare any single expense in your personal budget you multiply the monthly amount (found on page 13 of this book) by 12 (months) to determine your annual budget.

Evaluate the following items: Housing, Clothing, Transportation

How do your budgets compare with the national average figures? Note where your budget is either higher or lower than the chart by more than 20%. What might be the reasons for the difference? Write your thoughts on these similarities and differences below.

YOUR FAMILY SIZE _____

	A Your Budget	B Chart Budget (National Average)	C Your Percentage of the National Average	EXPLANATION OF THE DIFFERENCE
Housing				
Clothing				
Transportation				

Formula: A ÷ B = C

Group Brainstorm — Hard Times Budget

1. Review pages 95-96 in **Career Choices**. Sometimes it may be necessary to reduce your budget or "tighten your belt."

   Make a list of all the reasons you can think of that would require you to live on less money.

   1. _____   6. _____

   2. _____   7. _____

   3. _____   8 _____

   4. _____   9. _____

   5. _____   10. _____

Taking a Pay Cut

Hard times have hit the defense industry in which you work. The bill funding a large government contract anticipated by your company was defeated on the Senate floor. To balance the budget of the company and avoid lay-offs, the employees vote to take a 25% reduction in pay. Let's assume you make the salary you require for your desired lifestyle (the figure from page 87). You must now sit down with your budget and decide where you will cut personal expenses.

First decide how much money you must remove from your monthly expenses. Write the math formula and answer below.

Now enter that amount on the "Total" line in column B on the Planning for Setbacks worksheet on the following page.

Think about where you could cut expenses to meet this new lower monthly budget amount and enter those changes in each category in column B. Work independently using your own figures from page 13. Then, share your decisions with your classmates.

Living on Unemployment Insurance

The pay cut is still not enough to save the company. Within six months, the company goes bankrupt and must close its doors for good. While you look for a job, you must rely on unemployment insurance to meet your bills. Because you earned a good salary on your previous job you receive a total of $800 per month.

Complete column C on page 94 by starting with $900 as your total income for the month.

Planning for Setbacks

Category	A Your Budget Profile From Page 13	B New Budget Profile TAKING A PAY CUT	C New Budget Profile LIVING ON UNEMPLOYMENT
Housing	$ _____	$ _____	$ _____
Transportation	$ _____	$ _____	$ _____
Clothing	$ _____	$ _____	$ _____
Food and Sundries	$ _____	$ _____	$ _____
Entertainment	$ _____	$ _____	$ _____
Vacations	$ _____	$ _____	$ _____
Child Care	$ _____	$ _____	$ _____
Health Care	$ _____	$ _____	$ _____
Furnishings	$ _____	$ _____	$ _____
Savings	$ _____	$ _____	$ _____
Miscellaneous	$ _____	$ _____	$ _____
_____	$ _____	$ _____	$ _____
_____	$ _____	$ _____	$ _____
Total	$ _____	$ _____	$ __$900.00__

Describe how you decided which expenses could be reduced. Star (*) the line items where you could make cuts most easily. What changes in your lifestyle would be necessary in order to meet this new reduced budget? Use the space below to explain your decisions for lowering your monthly budgeted expenses.

Statistics — Developing Charts and Graphs

Charts and graphs are one way to see numbers in relationship to other numbers. **Circle graphs** are good to illustrate percentage statistics. **Bar graphs** illustrate comparisons of whole numbers.

Circle Graph

For example, below is a circle graph that illustrates the statistic *22% of American children live below the poverty level.*

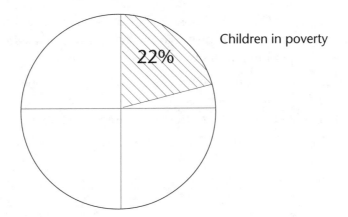

How to Draw the Percentage Representation

Start by dividing the circle into quarters. Use a pencil so the line can be erased.

Evaluate the statistic to be shown. For example, ¼ of 100 (whole) is .25 or 25%. 22% is slightly less than 25%. Therefore you would draw the slice of the pie to illustrate 22% as slightly less than ¼ of the circle.

Extra Credit

How could you be more exact?

You have been asked by the community organization you volunteer for to make a presentation to the City Council to urge support of a city ordinance to provide more low cost housing. Rather than rattle off statistics, in your presentation that no one will listen to anyway, you decide to make a strong and lasting impression about poverty by drawing some charts to illustrate key points.

Turn to page 103 in *Career Choices*. Choose one of the statistics listed at the top of the page and draw a circle graph to illustrate that statistic in relationship to the total population. Be sure to label your graph.

Hint: In light pencil — so you can erase the lines when you are done — divide the circle into four equal pie-shaped pieces, each representing 25% of the total. This will help you divide the circle to illustrate the statistic.

Draw a bar graph below to illustrate the difference between the weekly earnings of the three types of families described on page 103 of *Career Choices*. Remember to label each bar.

$1,200

$1,100

$1,000

$900

$800

$700

$600

$500

$400

$300

$200

$100

0

What do you find interesting or shocking about these figures? Write below your explanation of this graph as you would present it to the city council.

Form a team of 3 to 5 classmates to complete this project

What is Your Math Education Worth to You?

On pages 116 - 119 of **Career Choices** you worked through a problem that demonstrated graphically how important an education is to you in financial terms. On pages 211 to 213 you developed a graphic depiction of the differences between the salaries of jobs usually held by women and those usually held by men. Let's do something similar for your math education.

The Task:

Create a graph that demonstrates the long-term financial rewards of continuing your math education.

In other words, graphically demonstrate what staying in the math program and advancing in math will mean to your career and lifestyle options.

To do this you will want to compare the average annual salaries of careers that require only high school math, to careers that require college entry math skills, (Algebra I & II, Geometry) to careers that require advanced college level math (Calculus, etc.).

There are a variety of ways in which to accomplish this task so be creative and have fun with it.

Once your graph is created, make a presentation to your class about your findings.

Working As a Team

To successfully accomplish the task of creating your graph, you may want to review the following process.* Remember, in the world of work, time is money. Therefore, you want to be as efficient in your use of the time as possible.

1. Develop your system.

2. Evaluate your resources.

3. Decide on team assignments.

4. Gather information/materials.

5. Execute the project using technology for quality and efficiency.

First: Your group will need to develop the system for accomplishing this task. Meet together and brainstorm the different steps and components of the project. Develop a plan.

Second: You will have to evaluate your resources for accomplishing this task (time, money, equipment, information).

How much time do you have? Develop a timeline.

Will it cost anything to create? Write a budget and raise the funds.

What equipment will you use? Arrange for access to it.

What information is required? Check out the availability.

Third: You need to develop accountability within the group so you can work cooperatively and therefore efficiently.

Perhaps you want to have a chairperson, someone in charge of overseeing project coordination. Or maybe you want *shared leadership*. In this model, everyone knows their role and does it. Some people may be better at researching data, while others are better technicians and can draw or compute the graphs. Who will make the presentation? One of you, all of you, or a team?

Fourth: You'll need to gather and evaluate your data. There are a variety of ways to gather the data, so you'll need to choose the method that makes sense given availability and the skills of your group. When your research is completed, call a meeting for everyone to share their data and evaluate how and what to use.

Fifth: You'll probably want to use technology to produce your final project (perhaps the computer or special art supplies). The execution of the final project will require some form of technology, anything from pencil and paper to computerized imaging equipment. Decide what makes sense for your project and complete your assignment.

*Workplace competencies from the *SCANS Report*, U.S. Department of Labor.

Saving for Retirement

Review pages 208 and 209 of *Career Choices*.

We know it may be hard to think about retirement while still in school, but we hope the following facts will convince you that it is not too early to begin your savings plan for a secure old age.

The following chart shows the amount of money available at age 60 if you save $100 per month beginning at age 20, 30 and 40 and invested at varying interest rates.

Average Annual Return	Age 20	Age 30	Age 40
5%	$152,602	$83,226	$41,103
8%	$346,101	$149,036	$58,902
10%	$632,408	$226,049	$75,937

On the chart below make a line graph that shows this information.

Hint: Use a different type of line (solid, x-ed, dashed) for each line representing the age you started your savings plan. (See the legend in the box at the bottom of this page.)

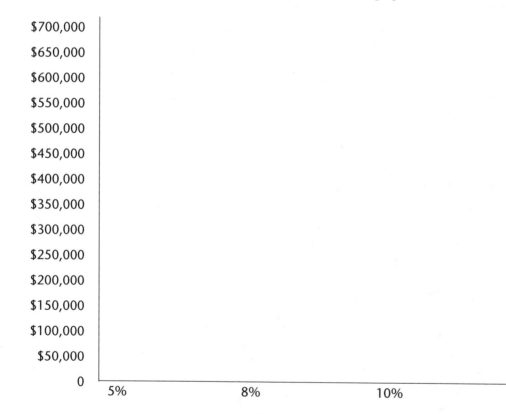

Amount of Retirement Savings Based on Varying Average Annual Returns and Age You Began

Started Saving for retirement at age:		
20	=	———————
30	=	x x x x x x x x x
40	=	- - - - - - - - - -

Extra Credit

What does the chart on the preceding page show you? Write your findings and assumptions here.

Given this information, what do you think would be your best plan for saving for retirement? Write that plan below.

Now look at the plan you have outlined. Is this a plan you could follow? Why or why not?

Inflation

You will need to use the library or an online calculator on a financial website to research the following data.

What is inflation? How will it impact your savings plan?

Extra Extra Credit

When you look at the figures on page 98 it is important to keep in mind the effects of inflation. Let's assume you plan to retire in 40 years. If the rate of inflation is the same over the next 40 years as it has been over the last 40 years, what will be the "purchasing power" of $100.00? Estimate as close as you can given the information available.

$100.00 in 20 __ __ will have the purchasing power of $ _____ in the year 20 __ __.
　　　　　　　　this year　　　　　　　　　　　　　　　　　　　　　　　　　40 years
　　　　　　　　　　　　　　　　　　　　　　　　　　　　　　　　　　　　from now

Developing an Action Plan

First read pages 186 to 190 in **Career Choices** and complete the exercises. This will help you learn how to write goals and objectives. The most successful and happy people are usually those who know where they are going and how they are going to get there. They have a plan and a way of evaluating whether they are successful. Most successful individuals use quantitative goals and objectives for the development of their plan. The word *quantitative* means measurable by a specific amount. This usually involves numbers or other units of measure (dates, times, weight, etc.).

The purpose of this activity is to give you more practice in writing goals and objectives and to demonstrate how useful this skill can be for helping you realize your dreams.

Let's develop a complete action plan for realizing a dream.

STEP ONE:

Decide what you want to accomplish or acquire. Write that in a measurable goals statement (as you learned to do in **Career Choices**, in chapter eight).

STEP TWO:

Brainstorm **all** the possible tasks that must be accomplished to meet that dream. Write everything you can think of. Once that is completed, decide what you must do to realize your goal by circling the **necessary** tasks from your brainstorming list. You now have the information to condense your list into tasks or objectives. (What will happen or be different?)

STEP THREE:

Develop a timeline. Place the steps appropriately along that timeline in the chronological order that they must be completed. For instance, if you are purchasing a car, you must first save the money or develop a credit rating so you can borrow the money. To save money, you must first have a job.

STEP FOUR:

From your timeline, write your objectives using numbers so you can measure progress toward your goal. Each objective must include:

        a. What will happen or be different

        b. By how many or how much

        c. By when

Objectives should be listed in the order in which they should be accomplished. If periodic check points would make the plan clearer and easier to use, indicate these by dates.

For example:

> To save my first $200 by March 31 of next year.
>
> To get a full-time summer job by June 15 that pays $7.00/hour.
>
> To save another $300 by June 30.
>
> To work all summer full-time and save 50% of my earnings ($1,000) toward my car.
>
> To save an additional $300 between September and December.

In this example, an individual can review progress every three months and quickly evaluate whether objectives have been reached. Then, if need be, they can rewrite or adjust their plan.

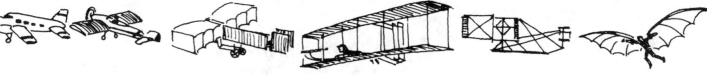

A Sample Quantitative Action Plan

Pretend that you and three of your best friends want to take a special vacation trip to some far-off place as a reward for graduation from school. You decide to go to Hawaii for one week during the following summer (11 months away). Here is what that action plan might look like..

Goal: To vacation for one week in Hawaii with three of your best friends during the week of June 20.

As you and your friends brainstorm the following steps, make them measurable and give them a deadline.

Objectives:

Meet with a travel agent and investigate the costs of a one-week trip to Hawaii by July 30.

Speak to your after-school employer and request an increase of four work hours per week by July 30.

Open a special savings account by August 1 and make monthly deposits.

Save your wages from the 16 hours of extra work each month for 10 months. (If earning $7.00/hr., that equals $1,120.)

Have lunch with your three friends once a month to report on the progress of each person's savings plan and discuss different vacation packages.

Read the Sunday travel section in the local newspaper to watch for "specials" to Hawaii.

Finalize travel plans no later than March 1.

Reserve hotel room by March 1 to get best selection.

Order airline tickets no later than May 25 to get lowest fare.

Can you think of any other objectives (measurable steps) you would add to this plan?

Form a group with 3 of your classmates and develop an action plan for the following goal.

Buying A Car

STEP ONE:

GOAL: To purchase a car a year from now. (Assume it is January 1.)

STEP TWO:

Brainstorm **all** the possible tasks that need to be accomplished before purchasing the car. List them below.

> HINT: You will need to consider money, financing, insurance, researching make and model, job to earn money, becoming a knowledgeable consumer.

Once you have listed every possible task you may need to accomplish before buying a car, circle the ones your group thinks are appropriate to your plan.

STEP THREE: Develop a timeline of the deadlines for accomplishing your tasks. Using this chart, list each task in the space to the right of the appropriate month. Use pencil so you can make changes if necessary. If you have any long-range objectives (i.e., earning the amount needed will probably take all year), be sure to break them into small units of time so you can evaluate them more easily as you work toward your goal.

TIMELINE

January

February

March

April

May

June

July

August

September

October

November

December

STEP FOUR

Using your timeline as a guide, write your quantitative objectives below in the order that they should be completed. Remember each statement should indicate:

   a. What will happen or be different?

   b. By how many or how much?

   c. By when?

Your plan for purchasing a car in one year.

Now It's Time to Dream

You are becoming an adult. In a short time you will be responsible for yourself and you hold the key to your own happiness and success. With careful planning and preparation, you can begin moving toward making your dreams come true.

If you could be ANYTHING you wanted when you become an adult, what would it be? Write that here.

_____

_____

_____

_____

Develop that into a goal statement below:

STEP ONE:

GOAL:

_____

_____

_____

Form a working partnership with another person in the class and work together to develop each of your own action plans for realizing your dream. Use the forms that follow. Once completed, copy your plan (page 110) onto a large poster board. Decorate the surrounding areas with art, clippings from magazines and other visual items that promote or remind you of your dream or the process of realizing that dream.

Share your project with your classmates and then take it home and hang it on your wall as a constant reminder of what would make you happy.

Each time you look at it say

I CAN DO THAT!

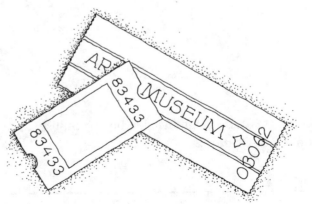

STEP TWO:

Brainstorm and list all the possible tasks.
Write them below.

Once you have listed every possible task that might need to be accomplished, choose the ones you think are appropriate to your plan. Circle those.

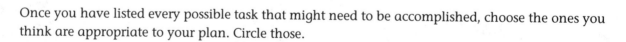

STEP THREE:

Develop a timeline of the deadlines for accomplishing your circled tasks.

THIS YEAR

March
|
June
|
September
|
December

NEXT YEAR

March
|
June
|
September
|
December

IN TWO YEARS

March
|
June
|
September
|
December

IN THREE YEARS

March
|
June
|
September
|
December

IN FOUR YEARS

March
|
June
|
September
|
December

If you require a longer time frame to realize your dream continue on another piece of paper.

Your Plan

Step Four:

Write your quantitative objectives below in the order that they must be completed.

The biggest reward of a carefully written action plan with quantitative goals and objectives is that you can step back, evaluate and enthusiastically say . . .

I CAN DO THAT!

As your direction becomes clear, your dream can become a reality!

Good luck!

May you become all that you are capable of becoming.

Mindy, Jo and Shirley

111

Other Books in the Career Choices Series

Career Choices: A Guide for Teens and Young Adults: Who Am I? What Do I Want? How Do I Get It? by Bingham and Stryker. 288 pages. Hardcover, ISBN 1-878787-00-4. Softcover, ISBN 1-878787-02-0.

Possibilities: A Supplemental Anthology for Career Choices, edited by Goode, Bingham and Mickey. Softcover, 240 pages. ISBN 1-878787-09-8.

Workbook and Portfolio for Career Choices, by Bingham and Stryker. Softcover, 128 pages. ISBN 1-878787-08-X.

Instructor's and Counselor's Guide for Career Choices, by Bingham, Stryker, Friedman and Light. Softcover, 408 pages. ISBN 1-878787-11-X.

For information on how you can obtain copies of the above books,
call Academic Innovations at (800) 967-8016.

About the Authors

Mindy Bingham is the author of 17 books with sales of over two million copies. She is the creator of the **Career Choices** Series which is dedicated to making learning relevant, challenging and fun. This math/financial planning portfolio for students has been a dream of hers for nearly 20 years.

Jo Willhite, M.B.A., has 30 years experience in finance and accounting as a controller and chief financial officer for small corporations. She also presents seminars in financial and personnel management. Interested in early childhood education, she has published a book on child care.

Shirley Myers, M.A., spent 25 years as a mathematics teacher, principal and adjunct professor of education. Serving on the California State Curriculum Commission and the statewide Mathematics Advisory Committee for 4 years, she conducted workshops for these organizations as well as in-services for the National Teachers of Mathematics Council.

The authors would like to thank the following individuals for their assistance:

Christine Nolt, book design and production; Michele Julien, editing and production; Betty Stambolian, Shirley Cornelius, and Nancy Marriott, editing; Itoko Maeno and Janice Blair, illustration; and Delta Lithograph, printing.

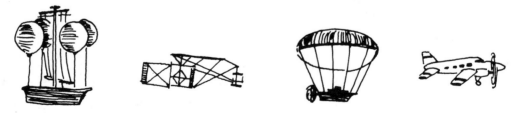

Illustrations: Itoko Maeno—1, 2, 3, 5, 10,11, 13, 14, 15, 17, 18, 23, 27, 34, 39, 40, 41, 43, 65, 66, 67, 71, 72, 75, 76, 77, 82, 83, 84, 85, 87, 88, 90, 91, 98, 99, 103, 108, 109, 110 111, 112.
Janice Blair—25, 30, 31, 32, 35, 36, 81, 92, 107.